IMAGES
of America

VERMILION
PARISH

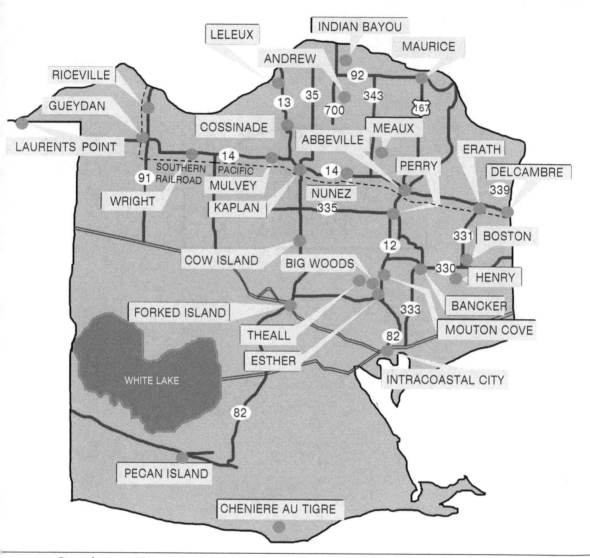

Over the past 250 years, waves of immigrants have arrived in what is now Vermilion Parish. These included French, Spanish, and Germans, as well as Acadian exiles from Nova Scotia. The Acadians' capacity to adapt and assimilate the other cultures gave birth to Cajun culture, which was also influenced by Afro-Caribbean elements. As seen by this map, early Vermilion settlers named their communities for animals, people, geography, and terrain. (Courtesy of Jim Bradshaw, of the *Daily Advertiser,* and Andrew Perrin.)

ON THE COVER: This 1912 photograph taken of the Whitney Pullin family is the earliest known photograph documenting use of the accordion in this region, according to Gérard Dôle and Dr. Louveau De Laguigneraye, French anthropologists from the University of Paris and experts in French/Cajun music. Shown in the photograph are Virginia natives and brothers Whitney (seated with his accordion) and George Pullin (standing, center), whose ancestors immigrated in the early 1800s to the hamlet of Boston in the area known as Prairie Greig (south of Erath). (Courtesy of Floyd Butaud.)

IMAGES
of America

VERMILION
PARISH

Warren A. Perrin

ARCADIA
PUBLISHING

Published by Arcadia Publishing
Charleston, South Carolina

Library of Congress Control Number: 2010939575

For all general information, please contact Arcadia Publishing:
Telephone 843-853-2070
Fax 843-853-0044
E-mail sales@arcadiapublishing.com
For customer service and orders:
Toll-Free 1-888-313-2665

Visit us on the Internet at www.arcadiapublishing.com

To my wife, Mary, for her loving support.

CONTENTS

ACKNOWLEDGMENTS

My mother, Ella Mae Broussard Perrin, deeply loved Vermilion Parish. Her death on April 20, 2006, was the inspiration for this book. Other influences were my lifelong friend Val Delino, who located previously unpublished photographs, and my cousin Una B. Evans, chairperson of the history book committee of the Vermilion Historical Society, which published *History of Vermilion Parish, Louisiana*, Volume I, in 1983.

Additional photographs were provided by Henri Deshotels III, Glen Viltz, Archie Chauvin, Sherry Hargrave, Dr. Harold Travasos, Shannon LaSalle, Nancy Toups, Steve Frederick, Elaine Broussard, Tony Mayard, Willie Ann Baker Lege, Mike and Andrée Stansbury, Stacy Bodin, Diana Ortemond, Gabe Duhon, Sabra Simon, Albert Luquette Jr., Idouma Harrington, Mark Poché, Loubert Trahan, Priscilla Delhomme, Barbara Alexander, Darrel Hebert, Judge Edward Broussard, Johnny Picard, Andrea Meaux, Davelyn DeMarcy-Norby, Bernie David, Virginia Stuller, Lee Bernard, Ronald Gaspard, Rufus J. LeBlanc Jr., Joyce Landry, Nora Lynch, Marcelle Tessier, Gunner Waldmann, Kathy King, Billie Wayne Broussard, Rayward and Joyce Landry, Mary Marshall Watkins, Ross Hebert, Dr. Paul Villien Jr., Natasha Villien Leger, Pat Campbell, Kaye Bernard, Mary Morgan, Natial d'Augereau, Claire Villien Bohn, Alan Broussard, Judy Choate, Frances Hebert, Paul Landry, Donald Sagrera, Roland Broussard, Chris Watson Jr., Romona Babineaux, Ashley Trahan, Brenda Desormeaux, and Ruth Broussard.

Responding to my frequent pleas for other types of assistance were Rodney Broussard, Daniel Broussard, Karen Leathem, Gary Theall, Chris Frugé, Malcolm Comeaux, Charles Sonnier, Chris Segura, Joseph Hebert, Ken Dupuy, John T. Landry, Dr. Ray LaCour, Charles Dill, Cheré Coen, Earlene Broussard, Dr. Shane K. Bernard, Larson Bodin, Jason Theriot, Brenda Trahan, Russell Gary, Dr. Carl A. Brasseaux, Laura Gaspard, Ryan "Toby" Bernard, Frank Maraist, Wade Mouton, Jean-Robert Frigault, retired Gen. Robert J. LeBlanc, and Dr. Florent Hardy of the Louisiana State Archives.

All author's royalties will benefit the Acadian Museum, which sponsors the Living Legend program, honoring those who promote Cajun culture. Unless otherwise noted, all images appear courtesy of the museum. Thanks to the museum's directors, Kermit Bouillion, Ron Miguez, Robert Vincent, Andrew Perrin, David Dronet, and Carlin Trahan.

Thanks to Darylin Barousse, Bobbie Ramer, Sam Broussard, and Bruce Perrin, who prepared the manuscript. But the person who gave me daily encouragement was my wife, Mary Leonise Broussard Perrin.

—Warren A. Perrin

INTRODUCTION

The history of Vermilion Parish is written in the lands of its farming, ranching, trapping, fishing, and mining areas. The riches of its land and waterways were important to the early economy. With easy access to the Gulf of Mexico, residents found good fortune fishing the waters for the abundant seafood. Joseph Beausoleil Broussard, the leader of the first Acadians to arrive in the region in 1765, was one of the founders of the cattle industry. Later, the railroad proved to be a tremendous boost to the business interests of the region. The discovery of oil and gas in Vermilion Parish in the early 20th century has been responsible for a large part of the economy of the parish. In the community of Henry, the creation of the Texaco Gas Processing Plant in 1942 signaled the beginning of the parish's lucrative relationship with the industry. Today, Louisiana remains one of the nation's top crude oil producers.

Vermilion Parish, incorporated in 1844, is situated hard against the Gulf of Mexico in the central, southernmost portion of Louisiana, known as the "French Triangle." According to the 1990 US census, the parish has the largest percentage of Cajun French–speakers in Louisiana. The English term Cajun is a corruption of the French word *Acadien*, which describes the people who had been exiled by the British from Acadia, now Nova Scotia. Their ancient French dialect is still an important part of the area's cultural makeup. Because of this Acadian heritage, Roman Catholicism has been the predominant religion in the parish. Cajun customs, beliefs, songs, stories, language, festivals, and foodways are expressions of the parish's history. Acadians were not materialistic in the modern sense. Acadian women frequently gathered to make *chow chow* (relish), *confitures* (canned preserves), or *couvertes piqués* (quilts) from *étoffe* (fabric). However, since World War II, these cultural markers have begun to die out. Over the last few decades, however, there has been a concerted effort to retain these unique cultural indicators.

Because of its bountiful natural resources, Vermilion Parish has always been a beacon for immigrants. While a majority of the residents trace their heritage back to the Acadian deportation, a mixture of nationalities and cultures is an unmistakable component of the parish. For example, the founder of Abbeville was a priest from France, the founder of Erath was a businessman from Switzerland, the founder of Henry was Danish, and the first settlers of Delcambre were from Spain.

The various ethnic groups that settled in the parish, however, did not always live in harmony, as evidenced by post–Civil War vigilantes. The civil rights movement in the 1950s sought to end the conditions of state apartheid. There were separate schools for white and African American children until 1965, when the Vermilion Parish School Board, while under threat of a forced government plan, voluntarily desegregated the system, allowing freedom of choice.

In the parish, politics have historically been rough and tumble. The election process has sometimes involved stories of "bull pens," which were all-night parties that lasted until the opening of the polls the next morning. A common practice in some areas was to allow drunken revelers to be escorted to voting booths, where they usually voted for the candidate who had provided the spirits and merriment. Also, many were illiterate, which allowed a proxy or commissioner to cast their vote for them—usually for the "right" candidate.

Although it is easier to identify individuals who stand out as remarkable members of the community, less recognizable are the ordinary figures—postmasters, store clerks, farmers, teachers, and blacksmiths. Some of the more striking personalities include the following: Sen. Dudley J. LeBlanc, the entrepreneur, politician, and advocate of Cajun culture; Denise Boutté, the beautiful actress from Maurice; Abbeville native Robert Angers, who founded *Acadiana Profile* magazine in 1968; Bernice Gera, who, in 1972, became professional baseball's first female umpire; James "Sandy" Pinkard, of Gueydan, who, in 1982, teamed with Richard Bowden to write many hit songs; Charlton Lyons Sr., considered the father of the Louisiana Republican Party; Amos Comeaux, from Cow Island, who is in the Musicians Hall of Fame in Nashville and at age 15 traded a cow for a fiddle; Karen Trahan Leathem, a Kaplan native and historian at the Louisiana State Museum; Dr. Preston J. Miller, who made house calls by horse and buggy but tragically lost a hand toiling on the land he loved; Dr. Howard Alleman, presently the longest practicing physician in the parish; and D.L. Menard, the twice Grammy-nominated musician who has entertained people the world over, including the president of the United States and international members of royalty. Two natives, Charles Frederick and Alexandre Dartez III, who served in the Civil War—its 150th anniversary was on April 12, 2011—will be remembered. On July 21, 2009, legislation introduced by Congressman Charles Boustany renamed the Erath Post Office in honor of Conrad "Snookie" DeRouen Jr., an all-American favorite son who was killed in World War II.

The name Vermilion Parish is derived from the Vermilion River, named for the reddish, or vermilion, color of its bluffs. The parish has many canals and 42 miles of coastline on the Gulf of Mexico. The area is fertile with a vast expanse of prairies dotted with moss-covered woodlands. Bayous and coulees wind their way through flat coastal wetlands and swamps. Louisiana not only has a state flower, the magnolia, it also has a state wildflower, the aptly named Louisiana iris. There are four species of Louisiana irises native to Louisiana: the Blue Flag, Copper, Zigzag, and Abbeville Red (*I. nelsonii*). The three former species are widespread throughout the southeastern United States, while the Abbeville Red is restricted entirely to Vermilion Parish in an area south of Abbeville. It was discovered in the 1930s by William B. MacMillan and was later described as its own unique species, which arose from a hybridization among all three of the more geographically widespread species. Ecological and genetic studies are currently underway to further understand this rare species, which is also Louisiana's only endemic plant—the only plant that is unique to the state.

The annual rainfall averages a hearty 54 inches. Because of the area's warm temperatures, it enjoys a long growing season; however, its low elevation makes it vulnerable to hurricanes. Since 1891, a total of 30 hurricanes have made landfall in Louisiana. The BP oil rig explosion of April 20, 2010, caused the worst oil spill in US history and delivered a double whammy to Vermilion Parish. Too far away to play a significant role in the cleanup, it suffered a 45 percent decrease in sales tax revenues, and the moratorium on drilling cast a dark shadow on the future of the industry.

Vermilion Parish is situated in the heart of Acadiana, a cultural region established by the Louisiana State Legislature on June 6, 1971, in recognition of the area's uniqueness, grounded in its "strong French Acadian–cultural aspects."

In November 1760, five years before the arrival of the Beausoleil-led Acadians, Fusilier de la Clair purchased from Attakapas chief Kinemo the lands bounded by the Vermilion River and the Bayou Teche, thus making 2010 the area's sestercentennial. The past 250 years have not been without pain or conflict, but the parish's birth in 1844 and progress through two-and-a-half centuries are potent reminders of this unique history and the value of adaptation. As every county in the nation inevitably has its roots absorbed into the American mainstream, Vermilion Parish stands almost alone in retaining its unique cultural heritage, where even the English sentence bows to the diagram of an ancient French sensibility.

One

ORIGINS AND
SETTLEMENTS

Vermilion Parish, located near
the center of Attakapas Territory,
was carved from what was once
the vast Territory of Orleans.
On April 10, 1805, the Louisiana
Legislature divided it into 12
counties, including the county
of Attakapas. Shown enjoying a
rare snowfall in Perry in March
1957 is Sidney DeMarcy, married
to Lucille Sorbet. Together,
they had the following children:
Hartwell, Ray Allen, Carroll,
Vivian, Marylin, Eleanor, Goldie,
Gloria, Helen, and Sidney.

There were several French immigration waves to Louisiana. The Colonial French (1699 to 1765)—friends of King Louis XIV, soldiers, and *coureurs des bois* (frontiersmen)—came seeking fortune. The children of Jean Bares, a blacksmith who came to Louisiana in the mid-19th century from Europe's Pyrenees region, are, from left to right, Louis, Rose Bares Moore, Jacques, Eugenie, and Germain. Living legend Sen. Allen Bares, a descendant of Jacques, from LeBlanc, represented Lafayette Parish in both houses of the legislature from 1972 to 1992.

In 1778, the Miguez family moved to Louisiana from Málaga, Spain. After the Civil War, Anaclet Miguez moved to the Leroy (La Butte) area from Iberia Parish. In 2002, the magnificent Miguez Oak in Leroy was inducted into the Live Oak Society. In 1983, local artist Elemore Morgan Jr. painted the tree and named the painting *Oak Shape*, which was purchased by Roger Ogden, who donated it to the Ogden Museum in New Orleans. Pictured here in 1901 is Leoday Miguez, a grandson of Anaclet, who was buried beneath the Miguez Oak.

African slaves were brought to Louisiana principally from Senegambia (West Africa). They greatly influenced the culture, language, and cuisine. In 1724, Louisiana institutionalized segregation when it adopted the Code Noir (Black Code), laws governing relationships between the races. At the time of the major flood of 1940, when this photograph was taken of unidentified African Americans, they were subjugated by Jim Crow laws, which prevented them from using public facilities.

Vermilion Parish was populated by Irish, Spanish, and Germans—such as the Toups, Schexnayders, Bartels, Ramkes, Fredericks, Ruperts, Hoffpauers, Saltzmans, and Vaughns—as well as Haitians, Italians, and Sicilians, all of whom brought with them distinctly different customs and foodways. Sam Russo (below), who arrived in 1905 from Cefalu, Sicily, is shown with his daughter Theresa, now married to Dr. Harold Travasos. Often depicted as a tropical paradise, the region is hot, humid, and vulnerable to storms.

Climate influenced every building decision. In order to prevent damage from flooding and termites, early settlers built houses on cypress blocks, which lifted structures off of the ground. They also made use of *bousillage*, an excellent insulating mixture of Spanish moss and mud. The outside walls were covered with horizontal cypress planks for protection from abundant rainfall. Early inhabitants, like James Henry Putnam (right) of Rose Hill Plantation, shown in 1908 with son Robert, utilized such building techniques.

To combat the heat, high ceilings and windows and doors for Acadian houses were arranged for cross-ventilation. Usually, wide galleries ran the full length of the front, and a steep-pitched roof provided room for storage or sleeping and cooled the house. Honoré and Laurence LeBlanc are shown in front of their historical house, built in 1845 in LeBlanc, now owned by George and Marilyn Crain.

People of English descent—like
the Kibbes, Edwards, Harringtons,
Hargraves, and Greenes—who settled
predominately in Abbeville often built
homes influenced by the Victorian style,
which was popular in the Northeast.
One of the most useful elements of
this style in Vermilion's warm climate
was the full-length front porch. Shown
in 1905 are, from left to right, Joseph
Everard "Evy" Kibbe Jr., an Abbeville
attorney elected mayor in 1938 and 1952;
Ralph Kibbe; and Dr. Presley Kibbe.

To protect against floods, early dwellings were
often built on a natural levee bordering lower
elevations. Rufus J. LeBlanc Sr., a geologist,
worked for the Mississippi River Commission on
the first project to study how ancient Pleistocene
and more recent deposits formed the landscape
features of the parish. Shown here are Rufus and
his wife, Alva Mae "Bede" Broussard LeBlanc.

In 1843, Rev. Antoine Mégret purchased land from Joseph LeBlanc along the Vermilion River where he established a church and the settlement of Abbeville. The parish continues to be predominately Catholic to this day. In 1985, Weldon Granger, an Erath native and nationally known labor lawyer, presented a pair of bronze mourning doves to Pope John Paul II on behalf of American Labor. Those pictured, are, from left to right, unidentified, Granger, Meryl Pryor, and Pope John Paul II.

Abbeville was patterned after the towns of France, Reverend Mégret's native country. He designed the town around a chapel and two large public squares. The name Abbeville came either from the fact that Reverend Mégret was from Abbeville, France, or from the combining of *abbé* (priest) and *ville* (town). While residing in Vermilionville (now Lafayette), Mégret died of yellow fever in 1853. Shown in 1910 is Arthur Broussard of Abbeville driving near the town square created by Mégret.

When Vermilion Parish was created in 1844, Perry's Bridge was named the parish seat. However, after two highly charged elections, the legislature changed it to Abbeville. A.J. Thomas Sr., of Welsh descent, came to Abbeville from Indiana in 1895 to establish the phone company. During the 1900 Galveston hurricane, he rescued Elita Broussard from Abbeville, and he later married her. His son, businessman A.J. Thomas Jr. (right), is father of Dwayne (left) and Tamara Suire.

The people of this area are hardworking and independent. Combining work with a love of good food made work more pleasant, so each farmer harvesting a crop had the most delicious meal possible prepared for his workers. At the table in July 1960 are, from left to right, Ronald Trahan, Mary Ann Meaux, Bernadine Leger, Kenneth Leger, Ruby Menard, Gerald Menard, Lester Simon, Diane Duhon Simon, and D'Ella Simon.

The Vermilion River was the hub of economic activity, and dirt roads provided the daily means of transportation. Dirt or gravel roads connected smaller towns with Abbeville, making it the commercial center. In 1912, a tax was passed to build the Abbeville Highway, now officially named the Vermilion Parkway. Shown is Elito LeBlanc, the founder of Erath Farm Supply, with his mules and *traîneaux* (sled), which was used to pull cars out of the mud.

Other settlers arrived from Canada. In 1899, Rev. Fabian Laforest, a French Canadian priest, came to serve at St. Mary Magdalen Catholic Church in Abbeville. Members of his family followed him from Canada and settled in Vermilion Parish. Pictured in the early 20th century are his relatives, the four LaCasse sisters, born of the marriage between Louis LaCasse and Amanda Laforest, visiting in the Gordy home in Abbeville. From left to right are Adeline Virginie Stuller (seated), Albertine Gordy, Amanda Hebert, and Leontine Theriot.

16

Two

THE ACADIAN DIASPORA

Alexis Aucoin (L) and Obeal "Barlo" LeBlanc (R).
Photograph by Junior Bourgeois, reproduced by
Kermit Bouillion

Before deportation, Acadians were the healthiest people in North America, as, for the most part, they isolated themselves from other groups to remain politically neutral and to avoid the military struggles surrounding them. This, in turn, reinforced their newly developing ethnicity and strengthened community ties. Therefore, Acadians in Louisiana—like Alexis Aucoin (left) and Abeal "Barlo" LeBlanc of Erath, pictured in the 1960s—differed from other French-speaking peoples of North America.

From 1755 to 1763, the British deported Acadians from Acadie. Since the Treaty of Paris prevented them from returning to the lands their ancestors settled in 1604, some Acadians, including ancestors of Aladin LeBlanc, shown, departed for Louisiana in 1764. Hundreds of refugees who had first been exiled to France landed here in 1765, but most did not arrive until 1785, when seven vessels brought 1,600 Acadians to Louisiana.

Unlike most Acadians, others who settled in Vermilion had not first been exiled from the British colonies. In 1755, the British captured many Acadians, but 86 managed to escape from prison by digging a tunnel. The leader of these militants was Joseph Beausoleil Broussard, who eventually led the first group of Acadians to Louisiana. Shown at Erath High School in the 1960s is one of his descendants, Numa Broussard (right), with student Gwen Moss.

The British viewed Acadians who avoided deportation as threatening because they carried out an insurgency aided by the Mi'Kmaq Native Americans. After Quebec fell in 1759, the Acadians found their struggle hopeless and surrendered. They were imprisoned for four years on Georges Island in Halifax, Nova Scotia. Shown in 1949 are Acadian descendants Joseph "Joe Pye" Dronet and Deussard Vincent on the front steps of Vincent's house in Charogne near LeBlanc.

In 1764, the Beausoleil-led Acadians petitioned Gov. Montague Wilmot of Nova Scotia to be allowed to depart for Louisiana. With unrest in the area, the problematic Acadians were allowed to charter a ship and leave the lands they had occupied for 160 years. This is a 1925 photograph of Anna Broussard, wife of Harvey Broussard of Rice Cove, with daughters Vivian (left) and Amelie—all descendants of Beausoleil.

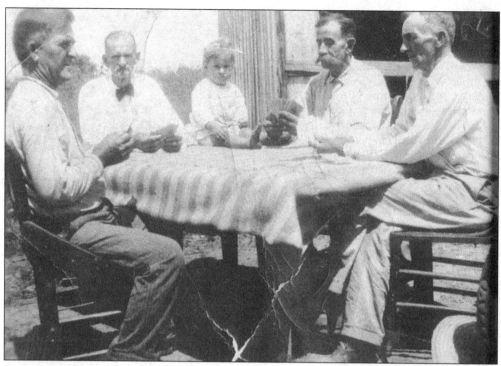

Fig. 4. The Bayou Teche, Opelousas area, and adjacent prairies of South-Central Louisiana.

In 1765, Beausoleil led the Acadians to Louisiana, which was then owned by the Spanish. They went to Bayou Teche and settled the Poste des Attakapas. New Orleans needed meat, so the Acadians negotiated a "sharecropping" cattle contract with Jean Dauterive, the owner of a large ranch near New Iberia. Shown is Demosthene LeBlanc (second from left) in 1890 playing cards with his friends, who were in the cattle business at Bayou Tigre. Note the Acadian homespun blanket.

In 1765, Beausoleil was named commandant of the Attakapas by the Spanish government, which awarded Acadians land grants. Sadly, Beausoleil never lived to see his dream of a "New Acadia" fulfilled, as he died of yellow fever in October 1765. To stop the epidemic, the remaining Acadians dispersed throughout the Attakapas region. By the 1770s, they had settled along the Vermilion River in Prairie de Vermilion. (Courtesy of Louisiana State University.)

Cohesiveness gave the Acadians the ability to endure discrimination. Early settlers, like Amelia Dyson (left) and Leveran Bourque of Pecan Island, acquired survival skills—such as treating illness with native plants, weaving palmetto leaves into hats, and farming local vegetables—from the helpful local Native Americans. Acadian men wore knee-length *braguettes* (pants), *cotonnade* (cotton) shirts, and *capots* (coats). Male footwear included *quantiers*, moccasin-type leather boots that reached to the knee.

The largest group of French to come to Louisiana was called the Foreign French (1820–1860). Dr. Lastie Maurice Villien (left) of Maurice and his niece Claire Villien Bohn, shown in 1962, are descendants of this specific group of immigrants. About 550,000 of these French immigrants came through New Orleans. They prospered because of their skills as carpenters, tradesmen, and farmers and were responsible for the emergence of French journalism, opera, and theatrical productions.

Resettlement to Louisiana was caused by political instability in Europe, which created widespread famine in France, thus stirring waves of migration in the 1820s. The people—mostly craftsmen and small businessmen who could no longer compete with the Industrial Revolution—became the store owners, shoemakers, and mill workers. Shown are, from left to right, Rixby, Edmée and Espéra Broussard, owner of a men's clothing store in Erath.

By 1900, having reached an accommodation with the natural resources, early settlers were on the threshold of a new period of sociocultural change. Diverse cultures in the region would come together to create what is now known as the Cajun culture. Shown are Amanda LaCasse Hebert of Abbeville and her three oldest children, from left to right, Henry Jr., Albertine, and Alice.

The Cajun culture consisted of unique crafts and music, which were passed on to children. Shown attending future–Living Legend Romana Stout Babineaux's eighth birthday party in Erath are, from left to right, Judith LeBlanc, Judith Dartez, Deanna Harrington, Nellie Ann Broussard, Gale Stout, Romana Babineaux, Charles Wren, Rosalie Landry, and Litia Ann Broussard.

The cultural transformation was determined by the capacity of the Acadians to adapt, as well as the willingness of the other cultures to be assimilated. This interaction contributed to the distinctiveness of the parish. The swampland—a haunting and mysterious place—seemed at first alien, but its abundant vegetation instead proved nurturing. Riding their horses in Meaux at the farm of Gaston Hebert in the 1930s are, from left to right, Edward Hebert, Daniel Hebert, and Leo Duhon.

Designed by Dr. Thomas Arceneaux, the Acadian flag features three silver fleurs-de-lis on a blue field, symbolizing the Acadians' French heritage; a gold castle on red, symbolizing Spanish rule; and a gold star on white, representing Our Lady of the Assumption, patron saint of the Acadians. The flag was unveiled on February 22, 1965, by, from left to right, Arceneaux, state comptroller Roy Theriot Sr. of Abbeville, and Judge Allen Babineaux. It was made official by Louisiana in 1974.

In 1990, attorney Warren A. Perrin filed a petition for an apology on behalf of all Acadians against the British Crown for wrongs that occurred during the Acadian exile. On December 9, 2003, Queen Elizabeth II's representative, Adrian Clarkson, the governor general of Canada, signed the Royal Proclamation, which is on display at the Acadian Museum, acknowledging the Crown's role in the deportation. The proclamation decreed July 28 an annual day of commemoration.

Three

TOWNS AND HAMLETS

Gueydan, in northwest Vermilion Parish, occupies part of an estate once owned by Jean-Pierre Gueydan of St. Bonnet, France, who left there in 1848 and was part of the Foreign French migration. The town, incorporated in 1896, became the rail center for rice farmers. Today, it is world-renowned for waterfowl hunting and annually hosts the popular Gueydan Duck Festival. Shown is Jason Campbell, of Delcambre, a champion duck and goose caller, at the world championship in Stuttgart, Arkansas.

Jean Maurice Villien was the founder of Maurice. His son Dr. Joseph Angel Villien Sr., shown here in the 1890s, graduated from Tulane Medical School in 1891 and practiced medicine in Maurice from 1891 to 1920. He was also a banker, businessman, farmer, and cattleman. He owned the cotton gin and the Villien Brothers Mercantile store in Maurice. Villien became Maurice's first elected mayor in 1911 and died in 1958.

Kaplan was originally part of a plantation owned by Jim Todd. In 1901, Abrom Kaplan, son of a Jewish rabbi from Russian-held Poland, bought the land and organized an irrigation company. O.H. Deshotels Sr., shown in the 1920s, helped to develop the town and established a general store and post office. He became Kaplan's first mayor. His son O.H. Deshotels Jr. was also mayor and Kaplan's first city judge.

Delcambre, whose namesake is Desiré Delcambre, has utilized its strategic location on Bayou Carlin, which leads directly to the Gulf of Mexico, to become a leader in the seafood industry. The first settlers, the Geoffroy, Miguez, Viltz, Rodrigues, Viator, Goutierrez, Segura, Romero, Gary, and Nunez families, were given Spanish land grants in 1790. In 1985, Patrick Campbell, principal of Delcambre Elementary School, is shown playing his accordion for a third-grade class while presenting a program about the town's history.

The Broussards, Pullins, and Hulins settled Boston. Rixby Dubois, of Boston, served on the Vermilion Parish School Board from 1956 to 1959. Nearby Henry was founded by William Henry around 1840. In 1996, Henry High School, the first high school in the parish, celebrated its centennial. Shown is 90-year-old Hattie Broussard, the oldest teacher attending. In 2005, Hurricane Rita caused the closure of the school.

Locally, coastal ridges, usually five feet above sea level, are called *îles* (islands). Île des Vaches (Cow Island) was settled around 1840 by Pierre LaPointe. On October 17, 1903, shown at the end of a long cattle drive from Cow Island to the stockyard in Abbeville—where the Broussard Brothers, Inc., building (formerly Riviana Foods) is located today—are, from left to right, Ernest Broussard, Joseph Broussard, Alan Broussard, John Walter Broussard, Alexis Langlinais, Alexandre Langlinais, and Ira Langlinais.

The Dyson family was the first to settle Chênière au Tigre (*chênière* meaning "oak grove") in 1840. Others to inhabit the area were the Whites, La Places, Broussards, Cessacs, Sagreras, Heberts, Rodrigues, and Choates. In 1913, Raphael Semmes Sagrera established the popular Sagrera Hotel on Chênière au Tigre, which is now a state preservation area. Shown here are Eula Choate (left) and her sister Eunice Choate Gastal.

Pecan Island was also a *chênière*, sprawling over three sandy ridges. In 1948, Pure Oil Company discovered natural gas while drilling one of the first offshore oil wells in Vermilion Block 39, about nine miles off the coast of Pecan Island. Shown in 1950 is the pipeline being built across the Pecan Island marsh to reach this historical field. (Courtesy of Tennessee Gas Pipeline archive collection, El Paso Corporation, and Jason Theriot.)

Meaux, located northwest of Abbeville, was first called Harrington's Island after cattleman Joseph Harrington. It was later called Millington, named after Millington Hartman. As with most unincorporated hamlets, the school was the anchor of the community and was built on land donated in 1919 by Michel Meaux and Odelia Broussard. Shown are early Meaux residents André DeBlanc (left), a *traiteur* (healer), and Guillaume Hebert, the father of Edier "Eddie" Hebert.

Shown is Chief Justice Frank W. Summers of the Louisiana Supreme Court, who served as an associate justice from 1960 until January 1979, at which time he was elevated to chief justice. He was married to Beverly Miller, and they had six children: Frank, Preston, Susan, Clay, William, and Beverly. His grandfather, George W. Summers, born in New Orleans in 1849, came to Abbeville to teach.

Bancker, located south of Abbeville on the Vermilion River, was once a bustling community with the following large plantations: Live Oak, Cade, Hope Mill, and Ramsey. In 1890, Diedrich Ramsey donated land for a school. In 1895, a Catholic church was established, but in 1939, it was moved to Henry and renamed St. John the Evangelist Catholic Church. Pictured in 1930 is the Bancker Grotto, which is maintained by Les Chretiens as a site for contemplation.

Four

WHERE MINORITIES
ARE THE MAJORITY

The Acadian community that emerged
from the turbulent Reconstruction
era following the Civil War bore little
resemblance to the stratified prewar
society. The postwar community
became essentially a two-tiered society,
in which status and wealth were
polarized between a small, educated
gentry and a large underclass. Shown
in 1907 is three-year-old Lillian "Sugar"
Cade, whose family owned Cade
Plantation in Bancker. She taught
first grade in Henry for many years.

By the end of the 19th century, many were forced to seek livelihoods away from agriculture in fields like fishing and trapping. Others were reduced to tenant farming. They would remain in poverty as *engagés* (indentured workers) until the industrialization of Texas's Golden Triangle—Port Arthur, Orange, and Beaumont—in the 1910s. This 1907 photograph shows Thomas Delino Sr. (left) of Henry, who left Vermilion Parish to work at Spindletop Oil Field in East Texas.

Members of the 1966 Vermilion Parish School Board are, from left to right, Leopold Noel Jr., George Veazey, Eugene Noel, Conrad Kaplan, Lovelace Hebert, Milton Reese, Gordon LeDoux, Superintendent Joe Kite, Pres. Peverly Broussard, Lionel Berry, J.C. Rogers, Ed Sigur, Dunice Meaux, Jill Picard, Dalton Domingue, and U.P. LeBlanc. In 1968, Judge Richard Putnam adopted the desegregation plan of the schools put forth by the school board.

Public education continued the cultural evolution. In 1916, compulsory education became the law. In 1921, the Louisiana Constitution mandated that only English be spoken in the schools. As a result of these changes, the Acadians would become a society in conflict with itself. Pictured in 1940 in Rice Cove (also called l'anse des Broussard) are, from left to right, Paul Asa Broussard, Ella Mae Broussard Perrin, Asa W. Broussard, Agnes Gautreaux, Adella Broussard, and Israel Champagne.

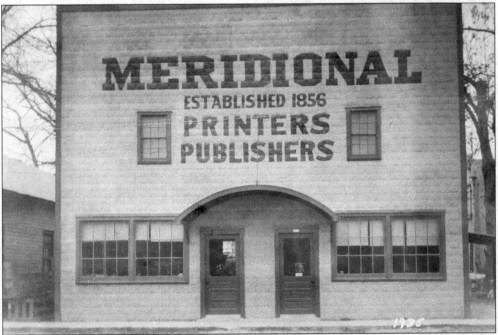

The parish's first newspaper was the *Independent*, owned by Reverend Mégret and launched in 1852 in French by Val Veazey. In 1856, the paper was sold to Judge Eugene Guegnon. He changed the name to *Le Meridional*, meaning "a native of Southern France," which Guegnon was. It was published in both English and French until 1866. The *Meridional* is the oldest continuously operating business in the parish. (Courtesy of Barton Bienvenu Collection.)

Initially, overland transportation was by horse or mule, but in 1880, the Southern Pacific Railroad completed its line from Texas to New Orleans. The railroad brought rapid change to the prairie landscape, bringing an influx of farmers from the Midwest and the beginning of the oil industry and agricultural mechanization. Demonstrating a method of breaking a horse by using two saddles and two riders are Paul L. Landry (left) and Ned Harrington in Perry in 1941.

Abbeville sought regional transportation, and the railroad accommodated. In 1892, the extension of rails from New Iberia to Abbeville became a reality. In 1902, the railroad ventured westward to Gueydan, which gave rise to Kaplan. In 1946, Lilly Romero Campisi, wife of Salvatore Campisi, of Sicily, is shown in Abbeville at Louisiana's first Conoco service station. The Campisis' son Larry served as Abbeville's mayor from 1982 to 1986.

Swiss immigrant August Erath founded the town of Erath in 1899. In 1910, Vernon Caldwell, Summa Caldwell, Damas Moresi, and E.P. Moresi founded corporations that are still in existence there today: the Erath Sugar Company, Ltd., Caldwell Lands, Inc., and the Bank of Erath. Vernon Caldwell was the bank's first president. Paul G. Moresi Jr., the bank's current president (pictured), led the bank's centennial celebration on November 18, 2010.

Prior to the civil rights movement in the mid-20th century, segregation was the norm in Vermilion Parish. Although they contributed significantly to local culture in areas such as music and cuisine, African Americans who dared cross racial barriers often faced violent, extralegal retribution. It was not until the 1950s that the first African American was appointed deputy sheriff, John Fuselier of Henry. Shown in the 1950s is Alcide Jessie of Erath, who was well known for making the tastiest cracklins (*gratons*), which are pieces of fried pork rind with some fat attached.

Dr. Shelly Mouledous attended Tulane University and received degrees in pharmacy, obstetrics, gynecology, and general surgery. In the late 1930s, he moved to Abbeville. He owned the Abbeville Pharmacy as well as the Abbeville Clinic, which he had purchased from Dr. Hartwell Eldridge. He practiced at the clinic until his death in 1975. Shelly was married to Josie Clements Mouledous.

Edward Joseph "Tee" LeBlanc was sheriff from 1932 to 1936 and was later appointed postmaster of Abbeville. His son Robert, who achieved the rank of brigadier general in the Louisiana National Guard, succeeded him. Shown in 1923 are Edward Sr.'s sons Edward "June" LeBlanc Jr. (left), who later in life obtained a medical degree and became a surgeon, and Robert J. LeBlanc, who is now a retired general. The brothers were both named Living Legends.

Arthur Sandoz had a long association with Gov. Huey P. Long, who was assassinated on September 9, 1935, and dominated local politics, in part because there was no civil service system to insulate government employees from inappropriate political pressures. The governor's powers to appoint persons to government jobs gave Sandoz tremendous control over parish affairs. Pictured is his son, Abbeville attorney Nolan J. Sandoz Sr., at Louisiana State University (LSU) in the 1930s.

Wells Fargo provided transportation before the railroad was built. Its building was constructed in 1897, one of four structures in Abbeville on the National Register of Historic Places. After the railroad came, people used the train to get to the parish since roads were in poor condition. In 1946, shown at the opening of Justin's Furniture Store in Abbeville are, from left to right, manager Justin Broussard, Ellis Trahan, and Leevan LeBlanc.

Although the majority of the settlers were French, Vermilion is a melting pot of cultures that evolved into a unique citizenry. In 1975, after the Vietnam War, many Vietnamese immigrated to Vermilion Parish under the leadership of the Catholic church, since Vietnam, like Louisiana, had been a French colony. Their total parish population is now approximately 2,500. Dr. Derek Nguyen, whose family arrived in 1975, was the 2010 Cattle Festival's Citizen of the Year, the first Vietnamese American to be so honored.

The parish has lost much of its marshlands (formerly its natural protection from hurricanes) due to man-made erosion. With a prediction of rising sea levels, low-lying areas of the parish remain vulnerable to storms unless corrective action is taken. Shown is the Acadian Museum in Erath after Hurricane Rita devastated the parish in 2005. Hurricanes Rita and Ike in 2008 and the calamitous BP well explosion of 2010 are cautionary reminders of man's role in protecting the natural world.

Five

THE LEGENDS
OF THE PARISH

Founded in 1990, the Acadian Museum of Erath began a program, under the directorship of Kermit Bouillion, that inducted persons who helped promote Cajun culture into its Order of Living Legends. On November 2, 2010, Bouillion was elected to the Lafayette Parish School Board. In October 1992, Bouillion is photographed in Lafayette with Arkansas governor Bill Clinton on a campaign stop before he was elected president.

Ned Doucet, a native of Kaplan, former state senator, and named a Living Legend, served as the chief judge of the Third Circuit Court of Appeals. In 2009, the judges on the court were, from left to right, (seated) John Saunders and Sylvia Cook; (standing) Billie Woodard, Jimmy Peters, Gene Thibodeaux, Mike Sullivan, Doucet, Oswald Decuir, Elizabeth Pickett, Glenn Gremillion, Marc Amy (of Abbeville), and Billy Ezell.

In the early 1900s, New York City children from impoverished families were sent to southern families by special trains called "orphan trains." Born in New York in 1916, Alice Bernard, an orphan train rider, came to Delcambre as a toddler speaking English. To communicate with the Auguste Geoffroy family, who had "ordered" her from their priest, she had to learn French. Ironically, she was later required to speak English, which she had forgotten, at school. She was named a Living Legend in 2002 and is pictured with her family. From left to right are (first row) Reuben Paul, Mary, Alice, Reuben, and Kaye; (second row) Glenn, Lola, Connie, and Ryan.

Richard J. Putnam Sr., born in 1913 in Abbeville, graduated from Abbeville High School and Loyola University School of Law. Putnam, married to Dorothea Gooch, was later elected district attorney and district judge. In 1961, Pres. John F. Kennedy appointed him US federal district judge for the Western District of Louisiana. Lafayette's Putnam Park is named in his honor. He was named a Living Legend on July 14, 2001.

LSU French teacher Earlene Broussard of Kaplan is identified with Théâtre Cadien (Cajun Theater). After studying French and Spanish, she served from 1992 to 1997 as director of Le Conseil pour le Développement du Français en Louisiane (CODOFIL). She was named Teacher Scholar by the National Endowment for the Humanities and received the Ordre des Francophones d'Amérique. Pictured in 1995 are, from left to right, Perry Waguespack, Earlene Broussard, CODOFIL president Warren A. Perrin, and president of the Québec National Assembly Roger Bertrand.

Kaplan has always been a center of Cajun culture. In 1969, Earl Comeaux and Ken Meaux created *Bec Doux et ses amis*, a bilingual comic strip on Cajun life. In 1998, aided by Thyra Montgomery and LSU law professor Frank Maraist, Comeaux published *Galeemacha*, a compilation of columns on Cajuns that had appeared in the *Kaplan Herald*. Shown is Octave H. Deshotels Jr., Kaplan's 10th mayor and first city judge (1972 to 1978).

Alligators were so abundant that they were outlawed and killed to safeguard the fur industry. Later, alligator skins became so desirable that they were nearly hunted to extinction. Now, they are protected, and landowners are issued a limited number of tags per year for harvesting the reptile. Pictured is Clifford Stelly with an alligator he caught in 1976. For many years, Stelly was manager of the Vermilion Bay Land Company Camp, located on the Boston Canal.

Fr. Fabian Laforest, later Monsignor Laforest, a native of Quebec, was pastor of St. Mary Magdalen Church in Abbeville from 1899 to 1915. He prevailed upon his widowed sister Amanda Laforest LaCasse to move to Abbeville from Michigan in 1903 to assist him as housekeeper. One of Amanda's five children, Adeline, married Gilbert Fitch Stuller, who is pictured at right in 1916. Stuller, a concert violinist from Oregon, later became a World War I Air Service National Army bombing instructor. They had one child, Dr. Gilbert Stuller II, who married Alma Branner Bowen. Six children were born of this marriage: Virginia, Matthew, Gilbert III, Jennifer, Walter, and Elizabeth. Matthew "Matt" Stuller (below) is a well-respected philanthropist and the founder and chief executive officer of Stuller, Inc., in Lafayette, Louisiana, one of the world's largest jewelry manufacturers and suppliers. His sister Virginia is the company's premier services sales director.

Gilbert Fitch Stuller II graduated from Abbeville High School in 1936. He served in the US Marines and was one of the first American troops to occupy Japan following the war. He graduated from Loyola University as a doctor of dental surgery. In 2009, Virginia Stuller (pictured), his daughter, served as cochair of the acclaimed international commemoration of the 250th birthday of the Marquis de Lafayette, a hero of the American Revolution.

Bernie David, named a Living Legend in July 2010, wrote the song "La Valse d'Anne Marie" about his Nova Scotian–Mi'Kmaq ancestor. He is shown playing the accordion in 2009 at the Mi'Kmaq-Acadian Cultural Festival, where he received his Mi'Kmaq name, Etlintoq Muin (Singing Bear). David, of Cow Island, is the first certified Louisiana Mi'Kmaq Aboriginal Status Person recognized by the Association des Acadiens-Metis Souriquois. Shown are, from left to right, Marie Rundquist, David and Hank Middletown, Dave Bell, and Vonda Laffin.

During World War II, German U-boats operated in the Gulf, and locals were recruited by the Coast Guard to patrol the beaches of Vermilion. *Collier's Weekly* magazine nicknamed them "Swamp Angels," the only members of a unit to serve the US military without leaving home. Although they never encountered Germans, they rescued 35 US airmen who crashed offshore. Shown in the 1940s, Swamp Angel Ignace David, of Cow Island, served with Warren Greene of Kaplan.

Benager Spell founded Indian Bayou in 1833. In 1886, George Hays donated land for its school. Pictured are graduates Ray Trahan, now president of Louisiane-Acadie, and Brenda Comeaux Trahan, director of St. Martinville's Tourism Department and the Museum of the Acadian Memorial, on their wedding day in 1965 in Leroy. The Trahans are leaders in promoting Cajun culture and the Grand Réveil Acadien (Great Acadian Awakening) to be held in October 2011.

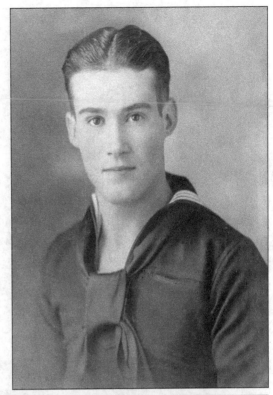

Dr. Alexander Sas-Jaworsky was born in 1916 in the Ukraine. In 1939, he lived first under Soviet, then Nazi, control. In 1951, his family settled in Abbeville, where "Dr. Sas" established a veterinary practice and was known for his outspoken political views. In the late 1950s, he is shown as a winning contestant in the category of American history on *The $64,000 Question* television game show.

In 1973, Gov. Edwin W. Edwards hosted supporters from Vermilion Parish at the governor's mansion in Baton Rouge to thank them for their help during his first gubernatorial campaign. Those pictured are, from left to right, Revis Sirmon, John T. Landry, Charles Sonnier, Edwards, Emery Sonnier, and Lee Pierce. In five decades, Edwards never lost an election and was elected governor four times. After serving more than eight years in prison for a corruption conviction, Edwards was released on January 13, 2011.

On February 17, 2006,
1st Lt. Brandon R.
Dronet was tragically
killed when a Marine
Corps helicopter crashed
off the coast of Africa
as part of Operation
Enduring Freedom.
Dronet, 33, a graduate
of Henry High School,
was married to Summer
Landry of Abbeville.
They had four children:
Duston, Courtnie, Cody,
and Madelyn. On May
30, 2006, a plaque was
dedicated to him at the
LSU War Memorial.

BERNICE GERA
First Lady Umpire

Bernice Shiner Gera graduated from Erath
High School in 1949 and umpire school in
1967. Facing gender discrimination, she filed
a civil rights lawsuit against the National
Association of Baseball Leagues and won the
case at the New York Court of Appeals. She
officiated at her first, and only, professional
baseball game on June 24, 1972. Gera is
memorialized in the Major League Baseball
Hall of Fame in Cooperstown, New York.

Shown is philanthropist Alphonsine Bares being honored in the 1981 Louisiana Cattle Festival Grand Parade for her financial contributions, which created the Bares Center in Erath. The center is sponsored by the Vermilion Association for Retarded Citizens and is now called the Arc of Vermilion. On June 1, 1980, a ground-breaking ceremony was held for the facility with the symbolic first spade of dirt being turned by Rev. Msgr. Rudolph Arlanti.

On March 21, 2008, Dr. David P. Manuel (pictured), an economist from Erath, was named the ninth chancellor of Louisiana State University at Alexandria. Manuel's research has centered on the energy industry, particularly its economic impact on coastal Louisiana and related public policy issues. Another well-respected educator is Abbevillian Walter Ledet of Northwestern State University. He was Abbeville's first All-American in football and later became a coach of both football and track and served as registrar at Northwestern.

Six

COMMUNAL
INTERDEPENDENCE

The *boucherie* (communal slaughter), when families joined together to provide meat for the week, was a unique tradition developed by necessity. When a pig was slaughtered, pork sausage and *fricassé* (roux-based stew) were prepared. These gatherings nurtured a sense of community, as did other forms of food gathering and preparation. Pictured is Sicilian Sam Russo's oyster boat, the *Imperator*, with Capt. Alfred Delcambre (far right), Russo (with necktie), and unidentified crew members.

The women's role in shaping the culture of Vermilion cannot be overemphasized. Women were influential landowners responsible for maintaining not only the family unit but also the farm, wealth, and religion. In January 1979, Sue Fontenot, of Kaplan, an energetic, bilingual, and tenacious attorney who graduated from Louisiana State University Law Center, was the first woman elected district judge in the 15th Judicial District. She died on July 29, 2008.

The preparation and enjoyment of food were relaxing pastimes for hardworking citizens. Roux, a browned mixture of flour and oil, provided the thick, robust body for gumbo, *sauce-piquante* (highly seasoned stew), rice dressing, and jambalaya. The Spaniards introduced spicy condiments. Those shown preparing boudin in the 1950s are, from left to right, Eunice Hebert, Clement Hebert, and Mrs. Dalton Sellers.

On October 23, 1902, R.S. McMahon and W.E. Satterfield drove from New Iberia to Abbeville to deliver the first automobile in the parish to Dr. Francis Fenwick Young. Allowing 10 minutes for oiling in Erath, the trip took nearly two hours. It was reported that Young, who had opened the Fenwick Sanitarium, did not like the car, preferring his horse. Charles Nunez of Abbeville is shown around 1910 working beneath his car, the "Leapin' Lizard."

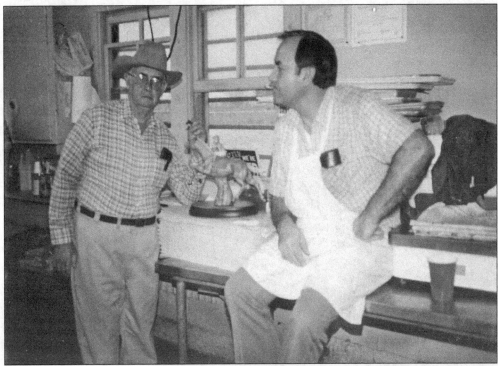

Around 1900, Eloi Hebert opened Cajun Downs, a "bush" racetrack where many successful jockeys began their careers, including Hall of Famer Kent Desormeaux. After Eloi's death, his son Clement Hebert (left) continued operations until the track closed in 2000. In 1955, Clement also opened Hebert's Meat Market, now run by his son-in-law Albert Luquette Jr. and his daughter Marjorie.

People often worked together in community cooperative events called coups de main (helping hands). Members of the Fa Tras band are, from left to right, (first row) Teddy Lemaire, Gerald Broussard, Mike Trahan, Willie Roy, Lynn Roy, Glen Touchet, Donald Borel, Minos Hardy, and Dave Baudoin; (second row) Johnny Credeur, Al Laviolette, Roland Broussard, Russell Gary, and Carrol LeBlanc. In 1983, the band performed at St. Jude's Hospital in Memphis and donated $5,000 to the institution.

Vermilion citizens often evacuate their homes before hurricanes to stay with relatives living out of the storm's projected path. Pictured are Richard and Mary Ann Broussard of Abbeville on their honeymoon in 1958. Before Hurricane Gustav in September 2008, the Broussards evacuated Abbeville for their daughter's house in Baton Rouge, but, ironically, the storm's path changed, and strong winds toppled a tree onto the house where they perished.

Shown is Mary Ellen McKay Sonnier, now of Abbeville, as Miss Washington Parish competing in the 1961 Miss Louisiana Pageant. While attending the University of Southwestern Louisiana, she also reigned as Miss University. Now married to attorney Charles Sonnier, she is a well-respected civic, religious, and business leader. She owns Magdalen Place, a special events facility, as well as the Depot, a historical railroad museum and gift shop.

After the 1927 flood, the US Army Corps of Engineers built the Atchafalaya Basin Protection Levee, causing diminished flow of water to the Vermilion River but exacerbating pollution. Today, the creation of the Teche-Vermilion Fresh Water District has improved water quality. Shown at its inception are, from left to right, unidentified, Carrol Fuselier, Gov. Dave Treen, Paul Begnaud, Dr. Harold Travasos of Abbeville, and executive director Donald Sagrera of Esther.

In the 18th century, 3,000 Acadians arrived in South Louisiana. They adapted well to the prairies and marshes and developed the cattle industry. Robert Broussard (pictured) was married to Ruth Bellamy and fathered Johnny, David, Rueben, and Tommy. Broussard and several families of Prairie Greig wintered their cattle on Marsh Island, where they maintained a community-owned camp. The cattle were transported by the *Mae West*, a boat owned by Aristide Broussard.

The whitewashing of tombs brought families together in preparation for la Toussaint (All Saints' Day) on November 1. Although the purpose was to maintain the tombs, it also involved graveside communal meals. Business trips usually took place only once per year to conduct legal matters and pay taxes. Staying at the Audrey Hotel was often the highlight of such trips. Shown in 1937, from left to right, are Bob LeBlanc, bellhop Thomas B. Delino Jr., Curtis Harrington, and Eugene LaBauve.

Seven

MUSIC AND
ENTERTAINMENT

The *bal de maison* (house dance) was an Acadian tradition. The accordion, the main instrument of Cajun bands today, did not appear until the late 19th century when introduced by German-Jewish retailers. By the early 20th century, a stock repertoire of Cajun music developed, based upon French, Acadian, German, Spanish, Native American, Scots-Irish, African, English, and American traditions. Pictured in the 1980s is Gueydan's Nathan Abshire, accordionist extraordinaire. (Courtesy of Elemore Morgan Jr. Estate.)

Dance clubs—like the Belvedere, the Airport Club, and Clems—were popular in the mid-20th century, but during Lent, Catholics refrained from such dances. In 1879, the *Abbeville Meridional* obliged the church by emphasizing penance in an article: "Balls will be discontinued now that the Lenten season has set in." Shown in 1939 competing in a Coronation Ball at the Silver Star Club in Maurice are Clarence Duhon and Laura Belle Bonin Hebert, wearing a dress she made herself.

Families would invite their *voisins* (neighbors) to a *veillée* (social gathering). Guests were served cakes, pies, *tartes à la bouillie* (sweet dough pies), lemonade, and home-brewed beer. *Bourrée* (a card game) was played by the men in a *cabine* (outbuilding). In the 1940s, Otto Baudoin (left) and Norris "Chin" Hargrave owned Otto's Bar in Abbeville, which was known for its card games. In 1950, Hargrave opened Chin's Corner Bar in Abbeville.

Mardi Gras brought communities together. Today, the Krewe of Chic-a-la-Pie (from the Mardi Gras song "Chique à la Paille"), originally formed as an all-woman group in Kaplan, carries on the spirit. Shown riding "Two Bits" in the 1930s is Rodney Simon, a prominent businessman who was married to Lorraine Domingues, and they are the parents of Kathy, Libby, and Denise. Simon died on February 15, 2011.

Soirées were evening parties where neighbors enjoyed a night of *rondes de danses* (five types of dance music in a designated order). The guitar, Spanish in origin, was important to local music. Warren "Storm" Schexnider, born in 1937 in Abbeville (shown in the 1960s), is a Living Legend of swamp-pop music, which is indigenous to South Louisiana. The genre combines New Orleans's rhythm and blues, country and western, Cajun, and black Creole.

Not everyone liked Cajun music. The Abbeville Playboys, a popular band consisting of four musicians from Abbeville, performed a combination of *américane* string music in French. Shown in 1918 are the Four Bangards, who are, from left to right, Myrtle Pate, music professor Ray Pate, Verna Pate, and Roy Pate. These Abbeville musicians played for American troops during World War I and also performed on Broadway.

During Lent, Catholics abstained from attending most dances; however, they believed dancing to music provided solely by the human voice was within the bounds of Lenten restrictions. Shown in 2004 are, from left to right, (first row) Jo-El Sonnier and Russell Gary, chairmen of FrancoFête 1999, Louisiana's tri-centennial celebration of the founding of the French colony; (second row) Ray Guidry, Jimmy Hebert, and Wilbert "Blackie" Foreman.

In 1922, Bourque's Furniture Company of Abbeville also sold Edison phonographs and records. The following are Cajun musicians: Harry Choates, Fenelus Sonnier, Isaac Sonnier, Cleveland Sonnier, Lanese Vincent, Sidney Richard, Milton Adams, Cedric Benoit, Lee Benoit, Jessie Leger, Ray Leleux, Klaby Meaux, Clercy Prejean, Joe Simon, John Dubois, Edward "T-Neg" Gaspard, Elias Badeaux, Otto and Wade Mouton, Eustis Champagne, and John Trahan. Lionel Leleux, shown in the 1970s, was a maker of fine fiddles. (Courtesy Elemore Morgan Jr. Estate.)

With the soldiers returning after World War II, Cajun music—a combination of old French songs, swamp pop, and blues—emerged as a symbol of ethnic pride. In the 1950s, Larry Brasseaux formed a group that performed a type of Cajun country music locally and in Canada. During the 1960s, the popular *Larry Brasseaux Show* aired Saturday afternoons on KLFY-TV 10.

Other musicians of the parish include Bob Brasseaux, Nelson Lange, Lynn Harrington, Joe Vice, Ed Landry, J.B. and John Peré, Jeffery Stelly, Eddy Raven, Steve Broussard, John Suire, Will Marceaux, Huey Meaux, Leewood LeBlanc, Donnie Broussard, Floyd Luquette, Earl Broussard, Clifford Touchet, Richard LeBoeuf, Shannon Suire, Fenelon Brasseaux, Sammy Kershaw, Ned Theall, Larry Menard, Gale Stout, Brandon Menard, and Michael Juan Nunez, who is shown performing in 1990 at Dee's Lounge in Abbeville.

D.L. Menard, Vermilion's most famous Cajun musician, was dubbed the "Cajun Hank Williams" at the 1973 National Folk Festival. His most famous song, "La Porte d'en Arrière" (The Back Door), remains a Cajun classic. D.L. and his Louisiana Aces have performed in 38 countries. His latest album, *Happy Go Lucky*, (Soileau Records, cover design by Megan Barra) garnered Menard a second Grammy nomination in 2010.

Popular in the 1940s, the Bamboo Grove Patio was located behind the Audrey Hotel. It was a circular-shaped hut made of large bamboo from Abbeville and served as an extension of the hotel's bar. Shown in the Audrey Hotel bar are, from left to right, Marion Hebert, Simon Primeaux, unidentified, Jack Brasseaux, "Buster" LaBauve, and Maggie Ewing.

Robert Charles "Bobby Charles" Guidry Sr., who died January 14, 2010, was a prolific songwriter. In the 1950s, according to Mike Stansbury, formerly of Abbeville, he and then-teenaged Guidry gained access to the African American–only club Robinson's Place in Abbeville and heard performers like Joe Turner, who influenced Guidry. Shown in 1996, from left to right, are Guidry, Sonny Landreth, and Sam Broussard recording "Goin' Fishing" at Dockside Studio near Maurice.

Female musicians include Judy Bailey, Shannon LaSalle, Lou Ella Menard (a Living Legend), Edith Trahan, Ethel Bourque, Inez Catalon, and Lula Landry (who both performed at the 1976 Festival of American Folklife in Washington, DC). Other women involved with Cajun music are Lillia LaBauve (director of les Petits Chanteurs Acadiens, formed in 1954) and Natial d'Augereau (director of Renaissance Cadienne, a folklife performance troupe cofounded in 1991 by Dr. May Waggoner). Shown in 1997 are young Renaissance performers Jessica d'Augereau and Jeremy Cook.

Pictured are the members of Renaissance Cadien, from left to right, Natial d'Augereau (Henry), Janine Dugas, Lois Theall, Harry Leonard, Connie Harrington Mire (Erath), Jack Rowe, Roger Cook, Lou Drouant, Willanna James, Haywood "Woody" Martin, Richard Hebert (Maurice), Steve Bing, Donna Bing, and Gisele Cyr. The folkloric group has developed a unique performance of 19th century songs and dances which they perform internationally.

Palmetto Island State Park, the first State Park in Vermilion Parish, located south of Abbeville in "Big Woods" on land purchased from Richard Wise, opened on October 28, 2010. The park is the culmination of 38 years of effort by John T. Landry of Abbeville, who served on the State Parks Commission and introduced the idea of the park in 1972. Landry married Sandra Broussard of Abbeville on December 17, 1966.

In August 1975, Walter and Effie Landry of Delcambre celebrated their 50th wedding anniversary with a French mass at St. Mary Magdalen Church. Philip Gould, then a young photographer pursuing his career in Dallas, documented the festive event. "This photograph of the lady with her indomitable spirit spoke to me. It became clear that I needed to return to work in Louisiana," he said. In 1996, Gould was honored with the Governor's Artist of the Year Award. (Courtesy of Philip Gould.)

In 1869, Joseph Dupuy opened Dupuy's Oyster Shop in Abbeville, using a sailboat to harvest his oysters. Dupuy's, still operating at the same location, is a multigenerational business now recognized as one of the 10 oldest restaurants in the state. Shown in Dupuy's in 1997 are, from left to right, R.J. Benoit, Ann Gaspard, Lillian Comeaux, Earl Comeaux, and Don Gaspard.

Dewey Segura, shown in 1986, was the second artist (Joe Falcon was the first) to record a Cajun song. In 1928, he and his brother Eddie of Delcambre, performing as the Segura Brothers, recorded the classic "Bayou Teche Waltz" for Columbia Records in New Orleans. Dewey, born February 12, 1902, was one of 12 children. His father was of Spanish origin and his mother French. Segura's wife, Euphemie, often accompanied him on guitar.

Riding in a *pirogue* (a long, narrow canoe propelled by paddle or pole) during the summer was a popular activity. The world became beautiful and restful in the tranquility of the parish's vast wetlands. Approximately the size of Rhode Island, Vermilion is the sixth largest parish measured by land area. This 1920 photograph shows Alphé Broussard (standing next to wagon) and his future wife, Odile Cade (standing next to wagon), herding cattle on Mulberry Ridge in a southern Vermilion Parish marsh. Seated on the front of the cart is Alphé's father, Joseph Broussard, and standing in the cart, from left to right, are Lillian "Miss Sugar" Cade, Camile Broussard, and George Broussard.

The relationship Vermilion Parish has with water is unique—sometimes entertaining or calming but at other times threatening and devastating. Retired lieutenant general Russel Honoré, a French-speaking Creole inducted as a Living Legend, is shown in 2005 in Erath supervising recovery after Rita. In his book, *Survival*, Honoré preached that houses that had been elevated prior to the storm survived without major damage. (Photograph by Susan Poag; courtesy the *Times-Picayune*.)

The crawfish is now a symbol of Cajun culture. Before 1950, crawfish were harvested only for individual consumption, but farmers soon realized the commercial opportunities and began flooding and stocking rice fields. In the spring, rice fields across the parish are teeming with people crawfishing. Shown at "Red" Richard's Crawfish Patio in 1970 are, from left to right, Diane Richard Frederick, unidentified, Ovey "Red" B. Richard Jr., and Florine Richard Vincent.

In 1886, the *Meridional* described Chênière au Tigre as "an attractive island several miles in length, covered with a beautiful and magnificent growth of venerable live oaks" where locals wintered cattle. In 1892, Eli Wise and James Henry Putnam bought a steamboat, the *Alice LeBlanc*, to transport the cattle. Shown in the 1950s are three generations of Putnams. From left to right are Robert Putnam, Mary Marshall Watkins, and Bobbie Putnam Marshall.

In 1880, an old building was purchased by Ivan Kuehling and moved to a corner near Esther in an area known as Little Bayou. In 1968, Robert Kuehling died, and artist John Bergeron leased the building until 1982 as John's Trading Post, a popular place for tourists who came to purchase Bergeron's books and paintings. Shown is Dalton Gastal, whose family was from this area.

Walter "Hobo" Campbell Jr. is pictured with his mother, Adonia Hargrave Campbell, of Forked Island. Hobo was a beloved Cajun of Vermilion Parish who operated the traverse (ferry) in Bancker and entertained passengers by playing the accordion and singing songs, including "Le Pauvre Hobo" (The Poor Hobo), from which he got his nickname. His grandson Dr. Brian Campbell is a professor of kinesiology at the University of Louisiana at Lafayette.

In 1985, Glen Pitre and Alan Durand filmed scenes of their movie *Belizaire the Cajun* on Harris Broussard's Pecan Island ranch. The movie depicted the vigilante crisis of 1859 as experienced by Belizaire Breaux of Vermilion Parish. Shown is Harold "T-Beb" Broussard (left), the former principal of Abbeville's Eaton Park Elementary School, on the movie set with fellow actor Michael Schoeffling. On March 25, 2011, the film's 25th anniversary, it was re-released in Lafayette in a new format.

Paul L. Landry, who has been in several movies, including *A Gathering of Old Men*, played the role of Sosthene in *Belizaire the Cajun*. He married Edola Margaret Perry, a descendant of the founder of Perry, 75 years ago. Others in the film were Gerard Sellers, Kala Chaillot, Rudy Faulk, Leroy Carter, Shelly Deshotels, Jim Nunez, Terry Perrin, Charles Broussard, Glenn Harrington, and Jimmy Meaux, who taught actor Robert Duval how to ride a horse.

Broussard's Bar was operated by Ovilier Broussard in downtown Abbeville. The men's establishment cooked meals for those working nearby. Shown in 1940 are, from left to right, bartender Ovilier Broussard; Billie Wayne Broussard, Ovilier's granddaughter; Clifford Broussard; and Claude Touchet. The beautiful rosewood bar is now in the Abbey Players building.

Photographed in 1995, attorney James E. Fontenot, the son of Kaplan farmer Tenes Fontenot, was elected state senator at the age of 27. He also wrote and directed plays and restored a historic hotel. Passionate to preserve French history, he served on the CODOFIL Board of Directors and hosted a program, *En Français* (In French), on Louisiana Public Broadcasting. Fontenot, an accomplished musician, died on July 23, 2004. (Courtesy of Ted Kibbe.)

In the early 20th century, teenagers enjoyed socializing at Cap's Place in Erath, next to the Bijou movie theater. The confectionery store was owned by Aurelien "Cap" and Etta Theriot. Shown, from left to right, are unidentified, Harold Broussard, unidentified, "Cap" Theriot, Velma Sonnier, three unidentified people, Zoe Dartez, Buck Jones, Nelwyn Lee, and Carrie Menard. After Cap's closed, the building was used as the town's library.

Pelissier Robert and Anatial Maitrejean married in 1888. Shown in the 1960s, from left to right, are three of their daughters: Louvenia "Bea" Robert Guidry, Edia Robert Gary, and Noelie "T Tit" Robert Menard. Other children of the marriage were Gaston, Edela, Marie, and Joseph. In 1911, after Pelissier died, Anatial married Clairville Broussard of Rice Cove.

Hunting has always been a favorite sport for those in the area. Most rural families had dogs to flush game during the hunt, and because rabbits reproduce rapidly, there was always an abundant supply. However, flooding from Rita in 2005 and Ike in 2008 took a heavy toll on the parish's animal population. David B. Dronet (left) and Vermilion Parish police juror Mark Poché are pictured in 1991 at the hunting camp of Burness Joseph "B.J." Gary.

Today, the LeBlancs comprise a 10th of all Acadians in North America. Joseph Aladin LeBlanc married Aurore Nunez. As was common in the 1890s and early 1900s, LeBlanc had to miss school to work on the farm milking cows, picking figs (*ramasser*) and cotton (*coton*), and working the *coupe de canne* (cane harvest). Children learned early that every hand was vitally important for the family's collective well-being.

In early schools, there were no lunchrooms. Children either brought their lunch pails, commonly filled with leftover rice and gravy, meat, and bread, or they went home to eat. This photograph shows Mount Carmel students around 1907. From left to right are Virginia Greene, Albertine LaCasse Gordy, Amanda LaCasse, Ida Bourque, Olive Cade, Adeline LaCasse Stuller, Marguerite Hebert, and Editha Goddard. Mount Carmel Convent opened its doors in Abbeville in 1885.

Alfred Moss, the progenitor of the Moss family and born in 1803 in Georgia, married Joanna Hartley of Vermilionville (now Lafayette). Today, Henry "Hank" Moss (pictured in 2009), the son of former sheriff Jack Moss (1956–1964), operates a ranch in Vermilion where guests from France come to intern. The cattleman learned to negate the effects of hurricanes by moving from a traditional cow-calf enterprise to a stocker operation, which involves buying calves and making a profit on their weight gain. (Courtesy of Mid-South Farmer.)

Eight

ART, CULTURE, AND TRADITIONAL CRAFTS

While most pioneer settlers gave up the practice of making *la cotonnade* (homespun cloth) upon arrival to the area, some artisans maintained their production. They became renowned for "Attakapas homespun," which came to the attention of national collectors. To produce their popular blue dye, they boiled indigo seeds. Those pictured in 1901 are the children of Thomas and Armezile Miguez. From left to right are Zeolide, Elena, Noah, and Zulmae.

During the 1920s, Cleomire Duhon Primeaux, wife of Severin Primeaux of Erath, was a prominent Acadian textile artisan. She kept a working area for her *métier à tisser* (loom) and *rouette* (spinning wheel) in the attic of her house. The fourth generation of her family to practice the textile craft, she was the subject of several books. Shown is Charles Primeaux at his Erath service station during the 1984 flood, fueling his boat so he can rescue people.

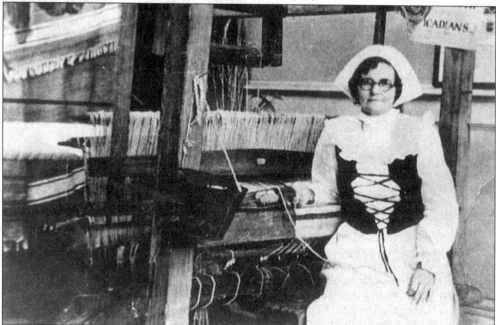

In addition to making their own clothes, women made *gardes-soleil* (sun bonnets) with *barbes* (shoulder-length sunshades). In 1929, a *courtepointe* (bedspread) woven by Thérèse Meyers Dronet, shown in the 1940s, was presented to Pres. Herbert Hoover. In the late 1950s, another was presented to First Lady Mamie Eisenhower. Gen. Curney J. Dronet Sr., author of *A Century of Acadian Culture*, is Dronet's grandson. The Dronets descend from Antoine Dronet, the son of Nicolas Dronet, of France.

Parish artists include Mae Mayeaux, John Bergeron, Steve Frederick, Tina Frederick, Nicholas Frederick, Gregory "Klebe" Meaux, Charlotte Broussard, Richard Suire, Mary Gutekunest Morgan, Becky LeMaire, "K.K." Herpin, Randal LaBry, Donella Hargrave, Greg Meaux, Jeannine Comeaux, Relie LeBlanc, John T. Landry, Mike Stansbury, Velta LeBlanc, Ted Baudoin, Florine Suire, Theresa de Perrodil Trahan, Tina Girouard, Bill Batic, Juliette Langlinais, and Warren "Tony" Mayard, shown painting *Swamp Spirits* for the Gueydan Museum exhibit in 2010.

The biblical phrase "ashes to ashes, dust to dust" produced an early folk religious practice, which became customary. According to Nicole Laviolette of Abbeville, after a birth, the umbilical cord was cut and a small piece left attached to dry and fall off. Once the remainder of the umbilical cord fell off, it would then be buried where rainwater falls. Shown in 1947 is Willie Ann Wilson Lege, of Grosse Isle, the granddaughter of Lucy Henderson Baker.

Elemore Morgan Jr., the father of Louisiana landscape artists, was a gentle giant of the arts. Vermilion Parish prairies, rice fields, and the big skies over them served as his constant inspiration. He worked continuously to promote the arts in Louisiana at Lafayette. His paintings of rice country in Vermilion Parish have been widely exhibited during a distinguished career as Louisiana's foremost contemporary landscape painter. Morgan spent 33 years teaching visual arts at the University of Louisiana at Lafayette and influenced students and fellow artists around him. In 2000, Morgan received the New Orleans Museum of Art's Distinguished Artist Award, and in 2001, he was inducted as a Living Legend. He died on May 18, 2008, and subsequently, September 18 was declared an annual "Elemore Morgan Jr. Day" by the State of Louisiana. Morgan's mother was Dorothy Golden of Abbeville. (Left, courtesy Curtis Darrah © 2007; below, courtesy Elemore Morgan Jr. Estate.)

As a teenager, Mike Stansbury exercised
at the Woodmen of the World gym in
Abbeville. In 1957, he formed a team at
Southwestern Louisiana Institute, which
won the National Collegiate Weightlifting
Championship. He established Mike's Gym
in Lafayette and hired Lloyd "Red" Lerille,
who later opened Red's Health and Racquet
Club in 1963. Shown in the 1950s are
Living Legend Mike Stansbury (bottom),
Cliff LeBlanc (middle), and Gene Hebert.

In 1981, Théâtre Cadien was formed
by Richard Guidry, Dr. Barry Ancelet,
David Marcantel, Amanda LaFleur,
Earlene Broussard, and Philippe Gustin to
encourage Cajuns to express themselves
in French. Others included Shirley Savoy,
Kermit Bouillion, Dee Doucet, Mary
Granger, Randall LaBray, Marjorie Toups,
Jane LeBlanc, Connie Duhon, Richard
Hebert, Rod Frederick, Christian Touchet,
James Fontenot, Tiffany Babineaux,
Scott LaPointe, Edith Trahan, and Allen
Simon (right), pictured in the 1950s with
Roland Simon, his nephew from Kaplan.

77

The Mandatory Education Act of 1916 mandated English in schools and began Americanization. However, in 1955, the successful state-sponsored Acadian Bicentennial Celebration became the genesis of the French Renaissance. The 1941 Meaux seniors are, from left to right (first row) Irene Légér, LauraBelle Bonin Hebert, Yola Montet, and Lorena Guidry; (second row) Harry Frederick, Oreste Miller, Roy Clark, Luther Faulk, Evelas Touchet, and Pervis LeBlanc.

The Anonymous Breaux Manuscript, the earliest existing local folklore commentary, notes that travelers requiring assistance during bad weather could seek shelter at any door. It also mentions communal projects, including the *piocherie* (hoeing party), the *couvrage* (shingling party), the *ramasserie de coton* (cotton harvest), and other demonstrations of community support—all forerunners of modern-day festivals. Dairy Day Parade participants are, from left to right, Mary Marshall Watkins, Mary Mathilde "Singsie" Putnam, and Deanna Comeaux Broussard.

On March 10, 2001, Louisiana superintendent of education Cecil Picard was inducted as a Living Legend. Picard, a native of Maurice whose father, Romain Picard, was an educator, had a major impact on Vermilion Parish education, serving as a teacher, coach, principal, state senator, and state superintendent of education. To honor his work in education, the University of Louisiana at Lafayette built the Cecil Picard Center for Childhood Development and Lifelong Learning.

Vermilion Parish people are a lively and colorful group; a sense of humor is a common trait that is expressed in both English and French. Many locals have amusing *tit-noms* (nicknames) derived from childhood events or physical characteristics—the Delcambre telephone directory is replete with them. Several examples are "Coco Ball," "Buckethead," "NuNu," "T-Gris," "Shoot-the-Bean," "Parrain," "Moose," "T-Bob," "Poon," "Zorro," and "Fiya." Shown here is Murphy J. "Mose" Boudreaux.

In 2009, under the leadership of Fr. William Blanda, a $3.7-million project restored St. Mary Magdalen Catholic Church of Abbeville after damage from Hurricane Rita. Ceiling murals, Stations of the Cross, stained-glass windows, and altars were all refurbished, and the iconic landmark was returned to its former glory. Pictured in 1950 are Abbevillians Rayward Landry and Florine Joyce LeBlanc Landry following their wedding at the church. The project was selected as a first-place recipient of the Louisiana Historic Preservation Award by the Louisiana Preservation Trust.

On January 31, 2010, Bishop Michael Jarrell presided over the rite of dedication of the newly restored Abbeville church. The first priest of St. Mary Magdalen was Father Francais (1848), followed by Fathers Therion and Mittelbronn (1851), Father Rogalle (1852), Father Foltier (1853), Father Poyet (1856), Father Lamy (1866), Father Méhault (1870), and Father Laforest (1899). Shown in 1959 are, from left to right, Sr. Mary John Seyler, Glenn Richard, and Sr. Denis Doughtery following Richard's First Communion.

In 2005, Acadians from Canada met with parish educators to help with French programs affected by Hurricane Rita. Shown in the Acadian Museum are, from left to right, (first row) principal Charlotte Waguespack, of Henry Elementary; principal Elizabeth Gremillion, of Dozier Elementary; principal Lynn Moss, of Erath Middle; and Rachelle Dugas; (second row) Gerald Boudreau, Ron Miguez, Warren A. Perrin, Michel Cyr, Zachary Richard, Roland Pautz, O.J. Dore, and Ray Trahan.

Paul LaPlace moved from Chênière au Tigre to 810 East Lafayette Street in Abbeville, where he established an oyster shop and grocery store. His son Buster helped harvest the oysters, haul them to the shop, and shuck them; he received three barrels of oysters as his share. Pictured in the 1930s is Ruby LaPlace Billiau, Paul's oldest child, riding her horse on Chênière au Tigre, formerly the premier resort of Vermilion Parish. In 2010, Ruby and Eluse Dugas represented Henry High School in the Erath High School homecoming parade.

Shown are two unidentified Mount Carmel students seated near Abbeville's Magdalen Square. The square is much different today, now bordered by a low brick wall and containing massive oaks, a fountain, a gazebo, and a statue of Abbeville founder Father Mégret. From the square, looking northeast toward the corner of Concord and Jefferson Streets, is the beautiful Bank of Abbeville, constructed in 1903, which replaced Gus Godchaux's old wooden store.

Artisans of the parish include Judge Durwood Conque (shown carving a duck in 1990), duck carvers Dr. Corbett LeBouef, Grant LeBlanc, Charles Robicheaux, and Earl Comeaux; seamstresses Egles Perrin, Laura Mae LeBlanc Romero, and Flo Hebert; David d'Augereau and Eli Choate, who made cypress pirouges (long, narrow canoes propelled by paddling); horsemen Ed Dugas, Robert Kasperski, "Hank" Moss, "Sonny" Moss, David Broussard, Bobby Bouget, and Harold Kuehling; crafters Mary Joyce Trahan and Joe Hebert; and photographers Leo Touchet and Peter C. Piazza.

Toward the mid-20th century, festivals replaced rural fairs. Shown are Bobbie Putnam Marshall (standing, left) and Yvonne Hebert DeGraauw representing Abbeville in the Crowley Rice Festival Parade in the early 1940s. In 1949, Roy R. Theriot Sr., the husband of Helen Roberts, organized the Dairy Day Festival, now known as the Cattle Festival. On Theriot's birthday, June 26, 1999, his children, Barbara, Roy Jr., and Sammy, donated his memorabilia to the Acadian Museum of Erath.

Candles were an important part of religious rituals. After a death, clocks were stopped, and coffins were shrouded in black for adults and in white for children. Candles illuminated the body, which was placed with feet toward the door and covered with *moustiquaire* (netting) to keep flies away. Pictured in 1921 with her First Communion candle is Effie Broussard. In 1925, Effie married Edier Bares at age 13 in this same dress.

This photograph of the Vermilion Parish Courthouse, found in the Louisiana State Archives by state archivist Dr. Florent Hardy, was taken by John B. Gasquet, who documented events for the Louisiana Department of Agriculture. The courthouse, designed by A. Hays Town with a distinctive Louisiana flair, was dedicated on May 30, 1953. (Courtesy of John B. Gasquet Collection, Louisiana State Archives.)

In the 1850s, bands of marauding cattle thieves roamed the countryside, and thus *comités de vigilance* (vigilance committees) were organized. An Abbeville ordinance required anyone selling beef to produce branded hides to show that the meat was not from stolen cattle. Granville Shaw, an award-winning sharpshooter who became sheriff in 1870 at barely 21 years old, was credited with ending widespread livestock thievery. He later became superintendent of schools.

Vermilion's writers include Sheila Hebert Collins, Jacques Couvillion, Dave Pierce, Gerard Sellers, Brandon Hebert, Richard Guidry, Gen. Curney J. Dronet Sr. (a Living Legend), Kenneth A. Dupuy, Russell Hebert, Leslie Hebert Helakoski, and Kevin Meaux. Chris Segura, of Abbeville, is an award-winning novelist, short story writer, and journalist, having worked on five continents. He is best known for *Marshland Trinity*, published in 1982, and is pictured during his honeymoon in Ecuador with the Tungurahua volcano in the background.

Members of the 1970 Vermilion Parish grand jury are, from left to right, (first row) Walter Primeaux, district attorney Bertrand DeBlanc, Mayor Young Broussard (Living Legend), James Giordano, and assistant district attorney Charles Sonnier; (second row) Elito LeBlanc, Emery Briggs Jr., Sidney J. Morvant, Galvey J. Hebert, Lee Myers, Thomas G. Baudoin, O'Neil Borel, Judge Marcus Broussard Jr. (a Living Legend), and Warren E. Broussard.

Living Legend R. Brady Broussard was the longest serving mayor—elected four times, three of those times without opposition—in Abbeville's history. In 1996, he hosted a reception in honor of a delegation from New Brunswick, Canada. Those pictured are, from left to right, president of CODOFIL Warren A. Perrin, Mayor Broussard, deputy minister Madeleine Delaney-LeBlanc, director Mirelle Cyr, clerk of court Sammy Theriot, and state tax commissioner Russell Gaspard.

In 1942, Aristide and Leontine Broussard leased 80 acres of their land for the construction of the Texaco Gas Recycling Plant in Henry. Today, Sabine Pipeline, LLC, owns the "Henry Hub." Here, 13 natural gas pipelines converge and 25 percent of the natural gas utilized in America is produced. The Broussard family is shown in 1905. They are, from left to right, (first row) Leta, Aristide, Lubria, Léontine, Rose, and Sulie; (second row) Nolia, Aliface, Ella, and Polycarp.

Renowned for his eggshell sculptures, Alexander Caldwell has a museum near Maurice. In 2010, the exhibit "Defining and Redefining the Art of Fabergé Eggs" opened at the Louisiana State Archives. In 2008, Emery "Bichon" Toups, founder of Abbeville's Giant Omelette Festival, was presented with one of the Fabergé-like Caldwell eggs entitled "Bichon Egg-Man." Those pictured are, from left to right, Elray Schexnayder, the third *grand maître* of the festival; Toups; and Caldwell.

Shown at the 1951 Southwestern Louisiana Institute (now the University of Louisiana at Lafayette) graduation are three members of the Hebert family. From left to right are James Duffy Hebert, retired library consultant for Jefferson Parish schools; Marguerite Frances Hebert, cultural activist and French teacher; and Charles Calvin Hebert, basketball coach and teacher in Meaux, Abbeville, Henry, and Erath. Their parents were Edier and Enes Hebert of Meaux.

In the early 1900s, three widely grown crops were rice, sugar cane, and cotton. Numerous rice mills, dryers, and warehouses were built throughout the parish. Initially, the grain was harvested by being hand-cut with sickles. The tractor-drawn binder, and, finally, the self-propelled combine replaced this method. In the 1950s, Jacques Noel (left) and Charles Dill Sr. are shown standing in front of the Vermilion Farmers Cooperative Association in Abbeville.

Pictured on June 3, 1952, is the Vermilion Parish Police Jury at the first meeting of the newly elected body. Members include, from left to right, (first row) Deussard Gaspard, Francois Detraz, Issac Lormand, Deussard Sellers, Eddie Hebert, and Adam Meaux; (second row) Emile Dutel, Edvar LeBlanc, H.P. Gurzardo, Saul Prejean, Nicholas Broussard, Leon Lormand, and Marcus Broussard Sr. (Courtesy of Vermilion Parish Police Jury and Marcelle Tessier.)

Phyllis Miller Taylor of Abbeville continued the work of her husband, Patrick Taylor, with the Taylor Opportunity Program for Students (TOPS) after his death on November 5, 2004. Now president of the foundation, she was awarded the Louisiana Endowment for the Humanities 2010 Chair's Award for Institutional Support. Shown at the 1949 Easter parade are, from left to right, Phyllis Miller Taylor, Linda Carlson, Connie Minvielle, and Claire Villien Bohn.

In 1830, Albert Stansbury and his wife, Eliza Ann Duncan, of Maryland, settled south of Perry, where they established a plantation. In 1916, Victor Schriefer acquired their house, shown here, and the area became known as "Schriefer's Curve." Family members seen on the porch are, from left to right, Victor, Ruth, Margaret, and Emma Schriefer. (Courtesy of John B. Gasquet Collection, Louisiana State Archives.)

Louisiana's 1808 Civil Code, influenced by the French Napoleonic Code and Spanish law, imposed forced heirship, thus allowing each child to inherit land equally. In other states, however, the law of primogeniture resulted in only the oldest child inheriting, thus encouraging out-of-staters to settle in Vermilion Parish. Shown in Abbeville in 1935 are, from left to right, Landry Stansbury, Mike Stansbury, and Beulah Stansbury of British ancestry.

There was perhaps no place else in the United States with people from so many racial, national, and cultural groups living communally. African slaves came with knowledge of tropical environments and agriculture. Despite their inferior social standing, they contributed substantially to the cultural *mélange*. Pictured in Abbeville are, from left to right, Mary Marshall Watkins, Agnes Jones (cook for Mathilde "Mattie" Putnam), and Kimball Marshall.

Nine

PUBLIC AFFAIRS, SPORTS, AND EDUCATION

Horses and cattle—the offspring of Spanish livestock that had migrated from Mexico—were already in the Attakapas when settlers arrived. Wild horses of the prairies and marshes were valuable assets for early settlers. Early in the 20th century, institutionalized horse racing became prevalent, growing out of informal races held on country roads or bush tracks. Shown at Clement Hebert's Cajun Downs following a race in 1976 is Clement Hebert, at the right of horse.

In the 20th century, the parish produced several excellent racehorses. Pictured in 1971 is Clement Hebert, located at the right of the man with binoculars, and friends, along with his son Doris Hebert, the jockey who rode Miss Margie H. to victory. Vermilion Parish is often called the "cradle of jockeys." On August 13, 2010, Randy Romero, a successful jockey from Erath, was inducted into the Racing Hall of Fame.

Vermilion Parish clerk of court Polycarp Broussard had a successful racing stable. Abbeville native Joseph "Spanky" Broussard Jr., pictured here, who married Florence Broussard in 1961, got his start working at Polycarp's horse farm. In 2005, he was inducted into the New Orleans Fair Grounds Hall of Fame in recognition of having won more than 85 stake races. Broussard trains horses at the New Orleans Fair Grounds and at Arlington Park in Arlington Heights, Illinois.

There have been many successful local horse trainers, such as P.D. Suire, Junius Delahoussaye, and Lloyd Romero, shown here. Romero, formerly a state trooper, began training horses after a car accident rendered him disabled. He became president of the Louisiana Horseman's Benevolent and Protective Association and was inducted into the Hall of Fame. Romero's most famous horse, Rocket's Magic, was featured in the 1978 movie *Casey's Shadow*, which was filmed in Louisiana.

Congratulations
KENT DESORMEAUX!
A WORLD RECORD
547
IN A YEAR!
From.
Laurel Race Course

Jockeys of note include Steve Soirez, Avery Mouton, Lester "Pee Wee" Gayneaux, Shane Sellers, Wilfred Bourque, Lane Suire, Ray Broussard, and Kent Desormeaux of Maurice (pictured), who has won more than 5,000 races. In 2004, Desormeaux was inducted into the National Museum of Racing Hall of Fame, and he was awarded the inaugural Bill Hartack Charitable Foundation Award in 2009. Since World War II, Cajun jockeys have won a total of 21 Triple Crown races.

The Caldwells descend from John and Margaret Caldwell, immigrants from Ireland. Abbeville's Caldwell House, built in 1908 and now a bed and breakfast owned by Mark and Darlene Frederick, is named for its builder, Vernon Caldwell (pictured). Caldwell co-owned a company that expanded into Caldwell Brothers Contracting, whose works include schools in Abbeville, Kaplan, and Gueydan. Caldwell served in both the Louisiana House of Representatives and the Senate.

For many years, the Meaux basketball team was a powerhouse. Team members are, from left to right, (first row) Hilton Abshire, Clarence Duhon, Davie Meaux, Joisey Faulk, Eves Simon, and Bernes Broussard; (second row) Melvin LeBlanc, Wilson Sellers, Weddley Meaux (the father of clerk of court Diane Meaux Broussard), Alexandre Bonin, Harold Meaux, and J.Y. Faulk. Raymond Larry Rupert was one of Meaux's most successful coaches.

In 1995, local teams won major championships. The 9- and 10-year-old Vermilion Biddy girls' basketball team won the world championship that year, and on August 19, the Abbeville 12-year-old boys' Bambino All-Stars hosted and won the 1995 Bambino World Series. Shown is the 1927 Maurice girls' basketball team. Team members are, from left to right, (first row) Onelia Broussard, Elena Hebert, Alta Picard, Leonie Vincent, and Gussie Nugent; (second row) Beulah McDonald, Melba Broussard, Edia Duhon, and Edes Clark.

Members of the Maurice High School basketball team, which won the Louisiana State Class C Championship in 1973, are, from left to right, (first row) Kim Broussard, Charles Broussard, Leon Broussard, Don Comeaux, Danny Broussard, and Virgil Vincent; (second row) coach Johnny Picard, Doug Picard, Arnold Trahan, Keith Sellers, John Houston, Larry Winters, Darrel Breaux, Pat Broussard, Eric Trahan, Dwight Girouard, Russel Guidry, Kenneth Trahan, and Bobby Duhon.

Two parish athletes were members of the University of Southwestern Louisiana's 1961 National Collegiate Weightlifting championship team, which included, from left to right, athletic director A.G. "Whitey" Urban, Gene Hebert of Abbeville, Gainer Burleigh, Rollie André, Weldon Major, Alvin Chustz, Richard Fleming, and Terry Perrin of Henry. Other parish weight lifters include Dwayne Thomas, Raymond Rodriguez, Kelly Perrin, Randal "Chip" Perrin, Malcolm Schriefer, Dr. Weston Miller III, Stafford Palombo, and Frank Motty.

Other Vermilion Parish members of the University of Southwestern Louisiana's National Collegiate Weightlifting championship teams were Mike Stansbury, Cliff LeBlanc, Andrew Hebert, Jay Trahan, Bill LeBlanc, and Warren A. Perrin. Shown is Bill LeBlanc, a 1967 Mount Carmel graduate. LeBlanc had a distinguished career winning major titles, including the 1978 US Junior National Championship. In 1995, he was inducted into the University of Louisiana's Athlete Hall of Fame.

In 2000, the *Meridional*, under the leadership of sports editor Chris Rosa, selected the parish's top 100 athletes of the 20th century. Shown are 35 of those 100 athletes who gathered at the Vermilion Catholic school gymnasium for this group photograph. They are, from left to right, (first row) Brenda Davis, René Trahan, Lana Broussard, Maisie Meaux, Dana Rudd, Anna Dartez Guidry, Dana Mouton Frederick, Sue Landry Touchet, Maria Romero, and Darcel Delcambre; (second row) Tommy Trahan, John Thompson, Howard Landry, Kevin Meyers, Jimmy Domingues, Edward "Parrain" Domingues, Tommy Broussard, Bill Gooch, Cordell Dartez, Neal Guidry, David Rogers, J.C. Rogers, and Larry Winters; (third row) David Perry, Warren A. Perrin, Joe Kite, Leon Ortemond, Ken Meyers, Eric LeBlanc, Farrell LeBoeuf, Billy Cormier, Mark Piazza, Paul Piazza, Eric Trahan, and Luke Harrington.

Pictured is Bobby Duhon, named by the *Meridional* as the 20th century's number one outstanding athlete of Vermilion Parish. At Abbeville High School, Duhon was a multisport All-State athlete in football, baseball, and basketball. In the late 1960s, he had a very successful collegiate career as quarterback for Tulane University and went on to have an outstanding professional football career in the National Football League with the New York Giants. (Courtesy of Bobby Duhon.)

The Louisiana Military Hall of Fame, under the administration of Louisiana's Secretary of State, opened on February 4, 2010, in Abbeville. Founding directors from the parish were retired general Robert J. LeBlanc, N.R. "Bubba" Broussard, Revis Sirmon (deceased), and Francis Plaisance. Executive director Paula Finley oversees the induction of military veterans who were awarded a Medal of Honor. Pictured during World War II is Living Legend Johnnie W. Suire (left) at Sheppard Field in Texas teaching English to French soldiers preparing for D-Day.

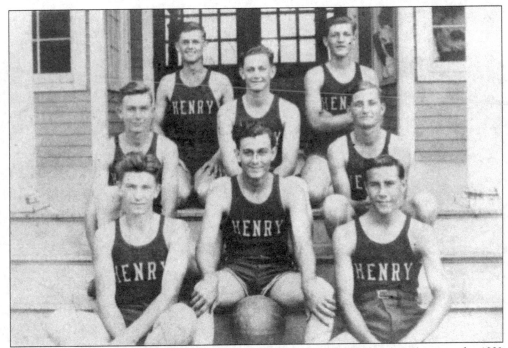

Activities like boxing, basketball, baseball, and track and field were popular. Shown is the 1932 Henry basketball team. From left to right are (first row) Clyde Lequeux, Elton Montet, and Thomas B. Delino Jr., (second row) Bill Ramke and Murphy Boudreaux; (third row) Verdis Butaud, Wilmer Domingue, and Douglas Hebert.

In the summer of 1934, Irene Whitfield and John and Alan Lomax came to Vermilion Parish to record Louisiana French folk songs for the Library of Congress. The Segura Brothers, with Eddie on fiddle and Dewey on accordion, were participating musicians. Pictured is the Stanley Gayneaux Band, with Living Legend Stanley (seated) and, from left to right, (second row) Joe Gayneaux, Curtis LeBlanc, "Junior" Bergeron, Edward "T-Neg" Gaspard, and Jack LeBlanc.

Revis Sirmon, shown here, spent his youth on a farm without electricity or running water. However, in the 1930s, he and classmate Roland Broussard left home to attend Louisiana State University. Later, Sirmon married Lorraine Breaux and had two children, Rebecca and Johnny. His 2009 memoir, *The Eternal Pilot*, chronicles his fascinating life from his days as a World War II fighter pilot to the meteoric rise of his business, Coastal Chemical Company.

The National Audubon Society's Rainey Sanctuary in Vermilion Parish is a 26,000-acre wildlife refuge. Since the 1950s, controversial mineral exploration has yielded $25 million for the society. Critics argued this made the society's opposition to drilling in other nature preserves hypocritical. Andrée Stansbury's 1970 photograph, entitled *Will Her Young Survive*, taken near the sanctuary, won the Photographic Society of America medal for Best of Show.

David Pierce of Intracoastal City was an All-State running back for Abbeville High School and is a Living Legend. He studied at the Pasadena Playhouse in Los Angeles, and he became a pioneer of FM rock radio, documenting the era in his book, *Riding on the Ether Express*, published by UL Press. Pierce cofounded the theater group Abbey Players in 1976 and the Woodlawn Players in 2002. He was part of the broadcast group that built Fox 15 and is now building SNAP and MUSTANG Radio.

In the mid-20th century in Vermilion Parish, the Democratic Party consisted of two factions, the Machines (Huey Long forces) and Home Rule (anti-Long forces). Animosity between the groups ran deep, and the bare-fisted politics spilled over and permeated every part of their social lives. Shown in 1994, from left to right, are Sheriff Euda Delcambre, a lifelong Home Rule member; Clifford "T-Cliff" LeBlanc, a Living Legend and noted cook; and Jimmy DeMarcay, Vermilion Parish sheriff's boat patrol.

A common political tactic used by both factions was "buying" commissioners who then "helped" illiterates vote. Another was the "bull pen," an all-night party where liquor was served to a group of easily influenced, unschooled voters. Sen. Dudley J. LeBlanc used his Sunday radio programs, sponsored by Hadacol, to influence listeners—mostly in French. Shown are, from left to right, Leroy "Happy Fats" LeBlanc, Al Terry, LeBlanc, and Oren "Doc" Guidry Sr.

Pictured at Police Juror Mark Poché's duck camp in 1994 are elected officials of Vermilion. From left to right are Erath constable Paul Poché, Erath alderman Carl "CoCo" Broussard, Henry Justice of the Peace Eric Toups, District Attorney Mike Harson, Poché, Judge Durwood Conque, Police Juror Ritter Trahan, Judge Edward B. Broussard, and Justice of the Peace Donald Mayard.

"Mr. I.M. Goldberg bought the Abbeville Athletics baseball team and struck a deal with the Vermilion Parish School Board to put up a diamond and stadium at Abbeville High School. One day, I went to a game and saw a beautiful young lady in a taffeta dress. With some persuasion, Nelson Frederick introduced me to Helen LaPlace who later became my beloved wife," said retired general Robert J. LeBlanc in his memoir. The LeBlancs are photographed in 1945.

Una Broussard Evans, who spearheaded the publication of *History of Vermilion Parish,* Volume I, and founded the Vermilion Parish Historical Society, was inducted as a Living Legend on January 12, 2002. Pictured at the event with family are, from left to right, (first row) Enix Broussard Lemaire and Evans; (second row) Warren A. Perrin, C.B. Vincent, Cleve Thibodeaux, Dennis Broussard, Edez Vincent, Pat Landry, Alfred Baudoin, Joyce Landry, and Reed J. Landry.

"As I stood on that stage on May 26, 1938, it was with pride that I accepted that diploma. At that moment, I realized just how much my father and mother had struggled through the Depression to see that we were motivated and understood the value of education," said retired general Robert J. LeBlanc. Shown is the first school bus (*transfert d'école*) of the parish and its driver, Louis Bares.

The parish's indomitable spirit has survived many tragedies. In 1867, Louis Delino perished when he volunteered to swim the flooded Vermilion River near Campell's Ferry to rescue its inhabitants. His body was never found. Those shown during the 1940 flood are, from left to right (seated) Cyril Hinckley, Antoinette Bernard, Dola Domingues, Velma Domingues, and Dorothy Landry; (standing) Della Bell Stout and D'Ella Comeaux; (on the porch) Santile and Otis Landry.

On November 12, 2007, the Keep Abbeville Beautiful Tree Preservation Committee and the Vermilion Historical Society donated plaques for trees on Abbeville's Donald Frederick Boulevard in honor of the parish's 11 World War II Abbeville soldiers and sailors killed in action. One of these sailors was Donald Frederick, who was killed when his ship, the *Arizona*, was sunk at Pearl Harbor on December 7, 1941. Nodily J. Faulk Sr., shown while serving in the US Army, was a teacher at Meaux, Erath, Henry, and E. Broussard Schools.

The 1960s brought profound divisiveness. Many baby boomers adopted political views—influenced by anti–Vietnam War protests—which often caused family splits. On February 9, 1961, prominent business and government leaders of Abbeville are shown enjoying a festive evening at the Blue Room in New Orleans. They are, from left to right, Ruth Broussard, Justin Broussard, Mayor Young Broussard (a Living Legend), Marjorie Boudreaux Broussard, Paul Piazza, and Felecie Piazza. The Piazzas' son Mark, married to Suzanne Harrington, is the present mayor of Abbeville.

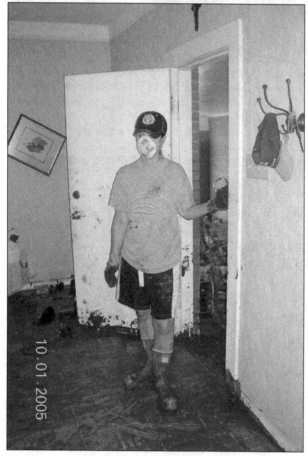

10.01.2005

John J. and Zoe Sagrera Lynch were lifelong conservationists and supporters of wildlife rehabilitation and the reestablishment into the wild of the endangered whooping crane. John was considered the father of "Flyway Biology," and Zoe, of Esther, operated Acadiana Marina on Pecan Island. In her 90s, Zoe wrote *My Memories of Chênière au Tigre*, documenting the island's history. It was published shortly before her death in 2010. Pictured are the Lynchs on their wedding day in 1941 in Henry.

Jennifer d'Augereau helped her family clean her grandmother Ella Mae Perrin's house in Henry after Hurricane Rita's 10-foot floodwaters had subsided in 2005. "Grandma could not find her pregnant cat and presumed she had drowned. But, later, we found a litter of kittens in an open drawer. The windows in the house had broken so their mother could enter as she pleased. Later, she moved them and we never saw them again," said Jennifer.

Members of a two-team, six-man peewee football organization at Mount Carmel School in the early 1950s were known as "the Fleas and the Flies." The purpose of the teams was to provide halftime entertainment at varsity football games. Flies pictured, from left to right, are (first row) Tony Hebert, George Sagrera, and Charles Sonnier; (second row) Rixie Hardy, Carroll Thomas, and P.T. Meaux.

Dr. Robert Hebert, a historian from Meaux who married Lilly Ann Vincent of Henry, was given the title President Emeritus of McNeese State University on August 27, 2010, after serving since 1987 as the fifth president of McNeese State University. He earned his doctorate from Florida State University and served as vice president for academic affairs at McNeese prior to becoming president. The Heberts have four sons: Greg, Chris, Gerry, and Edward—all medical school graduates.

After World War II, rural schools established "canning centers" to aid local residents in preserving foods and cutting and wrapping meats, eliminating the need for *boucheries* previously held weekly by many rural families. Shown is Joey Hebert, former agriculture teacher and principal at Henry High School, entering its canning center. Hebert later became superintendent of Vermilion Parish schools. He and his wife, Connie Broussard, were educators for 33 years.

Shown winning the 1975 Mr. Southern American title is body builder Glen Viltz of Delcambre. Body building in the parish had its beginnings at the Woodmen of the World Club in Abbeville, organized in 1895. Viltz owned successful health facilities in Lake Charles and Lafayette. Other enthusiasts of the sport were Darryl Guilbeaux, Richard Suire, Lenest Toups, Andrew "Refugee" Hebert, Kern Meyers, Malcolm Schriefer, Jack Rodriguez, Errol Broussard, Rudy Dronet, and Mike Stansbury.

The Women's Club of Abbeville was founded in November 1906. The service organization, known today as the Federated Women's Club of Abbeville, is responsible for the founding of the Abbeville Public Library. Shown at the Weill home after a meeting in 1951 are members, from left to right, (first row) Estelle Morgan Williams, Daisy Griffen, Gertrude Weill, and Bobbie Putnam Marshall; (second row) Mathilde Edwards, Mamie Sledge, Fannie Putnam, and Mamie Young.

In 1956, Fr. Emery Labbe was pastor at Erath's Our Lady of Lourdes Catholic Church and planned the racial integration of children's religion classes. This led to a violent confrontation where several white citizens battered catechism teacher Lula Bellanger Ortemond. The incident divided the community and was covered by national media, including the *Time* magazine issue of December 12, 1956. Shown are Lula Bellanger Ortemond (left) and her husband, Landis Ortemond, parents of Charles and Leon.

Shown are Jabian "Jay" Trahan and Rebecca "Becky" Broussard at the Mount Carmel Prom in the spring of 1964. In 1968, they graduated from the University of Southwestern Louisiana, with Becky earning a degree in home economics and Jay earning one in mechanical engineering. They married on January 27, 1968. While at Baker Hughes International and Oil States International in Houston, Jay was president of several divisions. Presently, he works in the industry with his two sons, Kevin and David.

In February 2010, the Abbeville High Schools boys' and girls' basketball teams won district championships. Shown is the 1963 basketball team that reached the state quarterfinal round. From left to right are (first row) Wayne Meaux, Mark Mouton, Ernal Broussard, Roger Boynton, Hampton Perry, Julian Hinckley, and Glen Hebert; (second row) coach Tommy Broussard, Bobby Duhon, Milton "Butch" Mouton Jr., Johnny Duhon, Ned Bond, Jimmy Moss, Harland Broussard, and coach Billy Gooch.

Ten

SOCIAL LIFE

In 2005, the Acadian Museum of Erath hosted a social for New Orleans evacuees of Hurricane Katrina. Shown attending are, from left to right, (first row) Debbie Bouillion; (second row) Jacqueline Hebert, Marianne Hebert, Carrol Hebert, D.L. Menard, Jarvis Hebert, and Paulette Hebert; (third row) Juanita Hebert, Beth Pizzeck, Kurt Pizzeck, Gladys Bourque, Mevaly Bouillion, Mae Delahoussaye, Louise Libersat, Edith Broussard, and Ella Mae Perrin.

In 1984, Emery "Bichon" Toups, Tracy Kays, and Sheri Meaux, members of the Abbeville Chamber of Commerce, attended the Easter Omelette Festival in Bessières, France, and were named chevaliers (knights). They then formed Abbeville's Giant Omelette Festival, hosting a sisterhood of Francophone entities, which include the following: Fréjus and Bessières, France; Nouméa, New Calédonia; and Granby, Canada. In 1985, the first festival cooked a 5,000-egg omelet, and every year an additional egg is added.

The Broussard family is the largest in the parish and has been instrumental in developing the cattle industry. Ernest and his son Joseph E. Broussard were owners of two of the largest ranches in Vermilion Parish. Joseph's son Alphé Alcide founded the Santa Familia Ranch, which is now the Flying J Ranch on Forked Island, managed by Charles E. Broussard. Charles, named a Living Legend in 2003, is shown in 1958 with his family. Pictured are, from left to right, Richard, Rose, Hal, Charles, Alan, and Yvonne.

Hebert is Vermilion's second most occurring surname. Joseph-Pepin Hebert arrived in 1766. His son François-Pepin obtained land along the Vermilion River, becoming a pioneer settler. On August 7, 1999, during Congrès Mondial Acadien (World Acadian Reunion), Abbeville hosted the Hebert Family Reunion led by Russell Gaspard (pictured) and attended by former New Orleans Saints quarterback Bobby Hebert, who was given a key to the city by Mayor Brady Broussard.

The Landry surname is the third most common and traces its ancestry to Acadians who came to Louisiana in the late 18th century. The first Landry in the Attakapas was Firmin. In 1775, his son Joseph married Marie Ann Melancon, and they settled on the Vermilion River. B.J. Landry (right) of Andrew, who won the first Abby Carter Award for economic development in 1999, is pictured with US senator John Breaux.

The fourth most frequent surname in the parish is LeBlanc, one of the most numerous Acadian families in the world. In 1801, Joseph LeBlanc married Marguerite Bernard, and their descendants occupied lands in Vermilion. Shown is Aldon "Shug" LeBlanc, who accidentally spotted his friend Jonas "Man" Perrin (left) on the street in Hawaii in 1944 during World War II.

Trahan, the fifth most numerous surname, comes from Guillaume Trahan of the Loire Valley, France. In 1776, René Trahan received a land grant along the Vermilion River. From Athanase and Michel Trahan, especially, descended two long lines of Trahans, many of whom by the mid-19th century settled north and west of Abbeville. Shown here in the 1970s are principal Earl Comeaux (left) and assistant principal Ritter Trahan of Kaplan High School.

The sixth most frequent parish surname is Guidry. This clan descended from a single progenitor, Claude Guédry dit Grevois. Seven Guidry families were among the group of Acadian refugees who arrived in 1785 from France. In 1791, Olivier Guidry married Victoire Semer, and by the 1850s, their descendants were settled in Vermilion Parish. This 1920 image shows Sabré "Pop" Guidry of Abbeville (sitting on the running board) with unidentified friends on a Sunday afternoon drive.

The seventh most frequent surname is Duhon. The Acadian Duhon progenitor was Jean-Baptiste Duhon dit Lyonnais of Lyon, France, who settled in Acadie about 1713. Church records suggest that before the Civil War, many Duhon families had moved into Vermilion Parish. Shown in 1956 is Slemco employee Claude "Pete" Duhon Sr. turning on electrical power for the first time to Pecan Island. Duhon also played stand-up bass for the Hackberry Ramblers.

The Meaux family is the eighth largest family in the parish. Shown is missionary Rev. Glen Meaux of Abbeville saying mass for congregants in Haiti. Haiti's recovery from a massive earthquake in January 2010 is progressing slowly, according to Meaux, who returned temporarily to Louisiana from his Society of Our Lady of the Most Holy Trinity mission in Haiti, which has taken in more than 1,700 refugees.

Romero, the ninth largest clan, arrived in the 18th century, when Spain was bolstering the population of its newly acquired colony. In 1779, six Romero families arrived, five from the Canary Islands and one from Málaga, Spain. Two brothers married into local French families, beginning their assimilation into French culture, which is a process common to most non-Gallic residents. Laura Mae LeBlanc Romero (right), a noted seamstress, was named a Living Legend in 1996.

The tenth most frequent name in the parish is Gaspard. The first Gaspard arrived from the Alsace-Lorraine region of France. R.C. Gaspard of Abbeville was state senator, and his son Russell was clerk of court (16 years unopposed) and a state tax commissioner. Shown in 1959 is Mount Carmel first-grader Ronald Gaspard. Ronald went on to become a bilingual private investigator and marketer of Good Old Cajun Seasoning and the Acadian Microwave Oven.

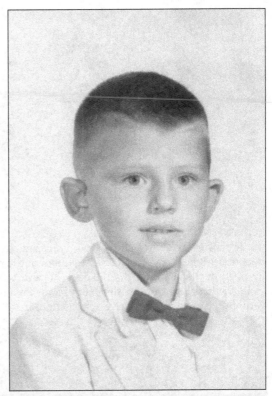

Richard is another frequent surname in the parish. The Attakapas District became the chief center of Richard families during the 18th century and remains so today. Two Richard brothers, Peter and Victor, began the clan here. Johnny Richard is shown surrounded by the saddles he repairs. He and his wife, Kathy Broussard Richard, also operate Abbeville's Le Bayou Legendaire, a unique venue for concerts. (Courtesy of Syndey Byrd.)

While crawfish is enjoyed throughout Louisiana, in Vermilion Parish it is celebrated. More than mere nourishment, the crawfish is a symbol of the region. Mounds of the 10-legged crustaceans are piled in the center of the table so that everyone is able to converse throughout the meal. In 1990, Patrick Stevenson (left) and Rufus Palombo are shown eating boiled crawfish at the Vermilion Farmers Cooperative Association in Abbeville.

An ambiance of vibrant good cheer characterized social life. Many local citizens enjoyed the communal atmosphere found in card games (*parties de cartes*), cockfights (*batailles de gaïmes*), house-raisings, and horse races—as well as the communal support accompanying them—and participated in such events year-round except during Lent. Shown are, from left to right, "Buster" Sandoz, "Monkey" Sandoz, "Buster" LaBauve, and Isidore Cabrol (holding rooster) following a cockfight—made illegal in 2008.

In 1971, Ed and Catherine Brookshire Blanchet became dissatisfied with the education their children were obtaining in public school, so they started their own. The schoolhouse in Meaux had four rooms and provided instruction in all 12 grades. Ed was trained in math and education, and Catherine (pictured in 1978) in music education, having written her master's degree thesis on children's songs of Vermilion Parish. (Courtesy of Philip Gould.)

On January 26, 1861, Gov. Alexandre Mouton, the first Cajun to be governor, presided over the state's Secessionist Convention. Alexandre Dartez III, an original settler of Maurice, was captured at the Battle of Vicksburg in 1863 and imprisoned for 18 months. He was reunited with his wife, Anastasia Hebert, on the steps of St. Mary Magdalen Church. In 1926, the *Meridional* published a series of articles about the Civil War experiences of Charles Frederick (pictured).

All Broussards of Louisiana descend from François Broussard, who was married to Catherine Richard in 1681 in Acadia. They were the parents of Beausoleil Broussard. By 1850, Vermilion Parish had become a hub of Broussard habitation. Chester Broussard taught at Abbeville High School and is shown with his family. From left to right are Winston, Gerald (whose wife, Kathryn, is the Vermilion Parish assessor), Barton, Chester, Melise Meaux, Claire, and Denise.

By 1810, there were 269 free people of color in the Attakapas region. Enmity between the races was apparent, but the prevalence of Catholicism, which spoke out against racial intolerance, buffered relations somewhat. Later in the area, Catholicism also impeded Ku Klux Klan activity, as the Klan was both anti-Catholic and anti–African American. Pictured here is Donald Moore of Abbeville at the Vermilion Farmers Cooperative Association.

In 1906, Frenchman Eugene Eleazar moved to Kaplan and on July 14 started the Bastille Day celebration, which commemorated the beginning of the French Revolution. Shown is the Deshotel family of Kaplan in 1908. They are, from left to right, Jeanne, Mrs. Leon Forest, Lelia Forest, Henrietta, Christine, Isabelle, Lucille, and Octave H. Deshotels Sr., the first mayor of Kaplan.

Raphael J. LaBauve (shown in 1910) was an attorney (*avocat*) from Abbeville who served as toastmaster for the 1913 Bastille Day celebration. LaBauve became an attorney by "reading" the law, which means he studied on his own rather than attending law school. The LaBauve family, originally from Brittany, France, immigrated to Acadia, from which they were exiled in 1755, and eventually, family members moved to Louisiana.

Sugar cane (*canne à sucre*) was first introduced in 1751 from Santo Domingo and raised on the plantation of the Jesuit Order in New Orleans. The C.S. Steen Syrup Mill has operated in Abbeville since 1910 and ushers in the fall season. *La cuite* is the juice of sugar cane boiled down to near-sugar. Shown cutting sugar cane in the 1950s are Landis Ortemond (top) and Julian Gayneaux.

For many years, Louisiana led the nation in wild fur production, and virtually all of the pelts came from the marshes. In the early part of the 20th century, especially during the Jazz Age, the parish's mink, muskrat, raccoon, and nutria pelts were in great demand worldwide. Shown is Thomas Delino Sr. at his camp in the 1940s, donning hip boots to go into the Vermilion marsh.

Because early legal descriptions of land used the French measurement of an arpent (about 193 feet), legal descriptions today often continue this tradition. Attending dirt-track horse races was a favorite Sunday afternoon pastime; the distance for these dirt tracks was seven arpents or approximately a quarter of a mile. Humorously pictured seated with his dog Rex on his horse Keto is Ferdinand Opta Villien in Maurice in 1914.

Thanks to the work of conservationists like Tim Creswell, there is hope for restoration of coastal wetlands and, thus, better parish protection from hurricanes and their dangerous storm surges. A former employee of Union Oil, Creswell became involved in coastal protection in the 1980s. Today, he serves the parish as assistant director of emergency management. On September 11, 2010, he was inducted as a Living Legend.

In 1918, the Erath Sugar Company needed local farmers (*petits habitants*) to supply sugar cane for its new refinery. This was the predominant reason the Grosse Isle, Prairie Greig, Bayou Tigre, and LeBlanc communities—established between 1781 and 1789—identified with Erath rather than Abbeville. Abbeville's Vermilion Sugar Company contracted with plantations along the Vermilion River to supply its cane. Pictured is the train used to transport sugar cane to the mills.

The citizenry of Vermilion Parish was predominately Catholic, and sacred and secular often intertwined, with the church's rituals frequently being the center of daily life. Public schools allowed students to receive religious instruction during school time. Pictured is the Abbeville High School band leading a procession of the newly inducted members of the Knights of Columbus to mass at the St. Mary Magdalen Catholic Church.

Shown in 1955 are, from left to right, vice president of the Vermilion Parish 4-H Club Allen Simon of Meaux; Lloyd Armentor, United Gas employee; and president of the Vermilion Parish 4-H Club Jackie Vincent Lemaire of Henry. Simon, inducted as a Living Legend in 1997, and Vincent were named outstanding 4-H students and were awarded scholarships to 4-H Leadership Camp Grant Walker.

Pictured are Emile and Ursule Dronet Broussard, who were married in 1860. They settled Aux Isles in southern Prairie Greig and reclaimed farmland from the marsh using levees as their ancestors had done in Acadia. The 1929 Depression changed the lives of farmers. Many lost their land, but those who did not went into subsistence farming, growing what was needed to survive, such as cotton, sweet potatoes, corn, and okra. Most had a small pasture and a milk cow.

Shown here in 1981 at the opening of the First National Bank of Abbeville, now Capital One, are, from left to right, Flo Hebert (commissioned to make the christening dress for President Kennedy's son Patrick, who died two days after his birth), Elizabeth Broussard Dugas, Nora White Trahan, and Gordon K. Marshall, the vice president of the bank. The First National Bank Building is on Charity Street located where the Robert Putnam house formerly stood.

Bob Moore, of Charogne, is the bilingual host of the morning television program *Passe-Partout* on CBS television affiliate KLFY-TV 10. On December 5, 1997, in honor of Fête de Noel d'Erath, a live telecast was held at the Acadian Museum featuring local personalities. Shown, from left to right, are Warren A. Perrin, attorney and museum chairman; Moore; cohost Gary Arnold; and Robert Vincent, who is now an Erath attorney.

Pictured is the Mount Carmel class of 1927. They are, from left to right, (first row) Anna Lou Duhon Bienvenu, Leola Frederick Dubois, Albert Kibbe, Earl "D.D." Broussard, Young Broussard, Robert Motty, Francis Broussard, Roland "Prof" Broussard, and Sidoux Webster Dubois; (second row) Renee David May, Louise Corner, Jessie Mae Lutgring Guchereau, Ruth Baudoin Miller, Cecile LaPorte Etie, Marjorie Broussard, Yvonne "Pud" Sigur Richard, Gertrude Frederick Thomas, and Sarah Broussard; (third row) Doris Barrilleaux Smith, May Yvonne "Badie" Baudoin Gooch, Audrey Mae Domingues Ledet, Lucille David Hensley, Theresa Campisi Betts, Maude Faye "Muffet" Baudoin Villien, Heloise Broussard, Clara Fleming Jett, Stella Thibodeaux Hollier, Cecile Broussard, Winona Schlessinger Morris, Lydia Piazza Abshire, Willie Mae Hebert, Marie Louise Hebert Hollier, Louise Broussard, Florine Motty Broussard, and Odette Bodin Ayers.

Visit us at
arcadiapublishing.com